The Holocaust

CAXTON EDITIONS
AN IMPRINT OF CAXTON PUBLISHING GROUP
20 BLOOMSBURY STREET, LONDON WC1 3QA

© CAXTON EDITIONS, 2002

ISBN 1 84067 295 1

A COPY OF THE CIP DATA IS AVAILABLE FROM THE
BRITISH LIBRARY UPON REQUEST

DESIGNED AND PRODUCED FOR CAXTON EDITIONS
BY POINTING DESIGN CONSULTANCY

REPROGRAPHICS BY GA GRAPHICS.

The Holocaust

Text by Professor Aubrey Newman

CAXTON EDITIONS

CONTENTS

Origins 7

The Nazi War against the Allies 43

The War Against The Jews 47

Concentration Camps 71

Jewish resistance and rescuers 111

Life in the Ghetto 127

Survivors Stories:
The Einsatzgruppen Killings 147

Survivors Stories:
Sara's Story 157

The Aftermath 179

Origins
1850-1933

IT IS IRONIC that the roots of the twentieth-century Holocaust which began by seeking to exclude Jews from European life are to be found in the very movement which sought to integrate them more closely into that life. The Emancipation process by which they were released from the brutal exclusion from which they had suffered for generations carried within itself the seeds of the hatred that found expression in the middle of the twentieth-century.

Until the growth of the Enlightenment of the eighteenth century Jews in Europe had been subjected to a wide range of restrictive practices and persecution designed to emphasise their lowly position in society and the community. The exponents of the Enlightenment saw in Jews a group that could be brought, eventually and after suitable 'education', into fuller membership of and participation in 'normal' society. It was not an easy process for either side, and there were occasions when the process appeared to have gone into reverse, but by the middle of the nineteenth century Jews in Central Europe seemed to have gained a degree of qualified acceptance within the State. The higher reaches of society, the upper levels of the professions, senior positions in the service of the State still remained closed to those who remained Jews, and sometimes even to those who had but newly converted to one branch or another of Christianity, but sufficient remained to satisfy many who now proudly proclaimed themselves Germans of the Mosaic persuasion.

Left: Jewish refugees from Russia arriving in New York harbour 1892.

The historic hatred of the Jews. Left: Blood libel. This 15th century woodcut shows Jews extracting blood from the infant Simon's body. Right: a woodcut from Schedel's Chronicle of the World, Nuremberg, 1493, showing burning of Jews.

There remained however a hard core of those opposed to such emancipation, and both economic and political problems which emerged in the Germany and the Austria of the fourth quarter of the nineteenth century led to the emergence of political parties proclaiming themselves openly antisemitic. In both states populist movements called for the repeal of all 'concessions' permitted to the Jews and for the restriction of rights within the State not only to those who were Christians but also to those who were of pure German blood. While in neither Germany or Austria were such parties in a position to influence Governments directly they could never be ignored, so that it could be claimed that in Germany by 1913 virtually every party had an 'antisemitic plank' in its political platform. It was an attitude which prevailed through virtually every aspect of the nation's life. In industry for example it was

Right: Sigmund Freud.

concepts as for example Sigmund Freud in psychiatric medicine.

Albert Einstein.

Emancipation in Eastern Europe had not proceeded very far; the Russian Empire had maintained its antipathy toward Jews, even though, in the Pale of Settlement – that part of Russia and Poland in which Catherine the Great had permitted Jews to remain after the various eighteenth century Partitions of Poland – they constituted a considerable element of the population. The economic discrimination represented by the May Laws of 1882 and the physical pogroms which were repeated often enough between 1881 and 1914 had for the most part reduced the Jewish population to the lowest levels economically and socially and attempts at Jewish self-improvement in the East more often than not found expression either in anti-Tsarist feeling or in concepts of nationalism centred elsewhere, such as Zionism. Yet detailed analysis of

striking that in 'big' industry, such as the making of steel, the old families, such as Krupps, very carefully kept out the newer families, including the Jews, so that they were much more often to be found in newer industrial activities such as chemical or electrical engineering. In academic or professional life the traditional strands of activity largely excluded Jews who were to show a pre-eminence in such newer

Jewish life in many parts of rural Russia and Poland finds a symbiosis between Jew and Christian. In many small towns there were even Jewish majorities, composed of artisans or merchants catering for a local market and creating important links without which the farming communities of the rural neighbourhood could not have survived. Many of the artisan trades for example continued till the eve of the second world war to be dominated by Jewish workshops. In the larger towns there were often to be found Jewish professionals, especially doctors and dentists; sometimes they had acquired their skills as part of the very small proportion of Jews permitted to enter the Universities, more often as a result of escaping over the borders into Germany and Switzerland to secure further education and training.

The First World War and the Peace Treaties which followed it had a massive impact upon the entire structure of Central and Eastern Europe. The disappearance of the great empires which had dominated the area left a number of 'successor' states with a multitude of problems and very little experience of finding solutions to them. These states had all been broadly based upon concepts of nationalism that had been laid down as the basis for a future structure of Europe. But within that state structure there were competing and unsatisfied nationalist ambitions, long rivalries between various ethnic groups, and a new significance given to issues of national minorities unable to join 'their proper' nation state and representing irreconcilable elements within the state to which they were allocated, and all this was complicated by largely inexperienced politicians and administrators trying to cope with the economic problems of a disrupted area. In addition, the peace of

Eastern Europe had been largely maintained by the balance between the three empires of Germany, Russia, and Austria-Hungary. The disappearance of two of those and the weakening of the third meant that the area as a whole had no basic stability, while the resentments felt in Germany by her loss of territories and the humiliations of the peace process itself ensured a continuing desire to reverse some aspect or other of the settlement. Perhaps the most intractable of all the minority issues was that created by the existence in Eastern Europe of a substantial Jewish population, everywhere in a minority and hardly ever felt by the local populations to be 'part of them'. In Poland, Hungary, and Rumania where the Jews were most evident feelings of animosity towards minorities were strong, and invariably accompanied by feelings of anti-Semitism. The new Polish state, reappearing after more than century of partition, was attempting to build a new national consciousness and to foster throughout its economic, social and political structure a feeling of 'Polishness'. Almost inevitably the Jewish minority was not felt to be part of that and the attempt to build up a Polish middle class meant that anti-Jewish measures came to be part of the state almost from the beginning. In Hungary, where Jews had to a considerable extent become assimilated into national life, the Magyars found that much of the Magyar population now lived outside a truncated state. Magyars returning to their homeland found themselves in bitter competition with Jews and there developed a strong anti-Semitic political movement within the state structure. Rumania, which had always shown itself very bitterly anti-Semitic, was greatly enlarged in its boundaries at the expense of the Hungarians and the Russians; having to build up a new massive governmental structure the government found it easiest to put the blame for all its difficulties upon the Jews who were, it was claimed, largely a foreign immigrant element. Behind all these issues were basic resentments in Germany and other states, dissatisfied with the Peace Settlements and determined to reshape the map of Europe at the earliest opportunity.

Exacerbating all these problems were fundamental issues of economics. The relatively integrated pre-war system of the Danube basin was not effectively replaced after 1919, and the growing world crises of trade created bitternesses. Above all in Germany the collapse of the German economy under the hyperinflation of the 1920s destroyed much of the basis of what political stability there existed. The Empire had been replaced by the Weimar Republic, but its enemies on the Left and the Right were determined to destroy it and its friends were neither strong enough or sufficiently far-sighted to be able to

Child using German Marks as building blocks.

counteract these growing menaces. Under all these circumstances, and with a desire to find a scapegoat for Germany's defeat and loss of territories, it is hardly surprising that in Germany too the Jews should find themselves the target of all the varied resentments to be found inside Germany.

One of the elements within the State

Top: The burning of the Reichstag, 1933.
Far left: Herman Göring.
Left: Hitler with President,
Field Marshall Otto von Hindenburg.

Above: Dr Joseph Goebbels at a demonstration in the Saarland in 1934.

Right: The Four Power Conference, between Britain, France, Germany and Italy, took place in Munich in September 1938. This last full scale diplomatic attempt to avoid war resulted in the Munich agreement. In the front, left to right are Field Marshal Göring, Italian leader, Mussolini, Hitler, and Italian Foreign minister, Count Ciano.

Hitler in Munich, surrounded by Nazi admirers shortly after he came to power in 1933.

seeking to take over authority was the growing German Workers' Party, soon (after it was joined by Adolph Hitler) to be renamed the National Socialist German Workers' Party. Avowedly anti-Semitic from its beginning this NAZI party invariably portrayed the Jews of Germany as the obstacle to all desirable change. 'If we wish to carry out these social reforms then the struggle must go hand in hand against the opponents of every social arrangement, Jewry.' Hitler's attempted take-over of the state by an armed uprising in 1923 failed, but within ten years the Nazis had become the largest political party in Germany, and in 1933 he was invited by the President of the Republic to become Chancellor and the head of government. The early years of the Nazi party had seen its adherents playing a violent part on the streets, beating up the opponents of the party, Jews and non-Jews alike, with comparatively little intervention by the police forces of the Republic. The party's advent to power saw the imposition from almost the beginning of a rule of terror. The burning of the Reichstag building was made the excuse for the abolition of all political parties other than the Nazi party itself and the Reichstag itself gave powers of legislation to the party machine. The creation of 're-education' camps, such as that established at Dachau, outside Munich, was the opportunity of removing from active political life all those who were deemed to be dangerous to the regime, Jews and non-Jews alike. But the steps taken specifically against the Jews included a call to boycott all Jewish-owned shops and stores, and this was to be officially enforced by uniformed members of the party, standing outside Jewish shops and warning the public not to enter. Another step was to remove from office those who were Jewish. This ran up against an obstacle almost immediately in that the President, Field Marshall Otto von Hindenburg, objected to the exclusion of those who had themselves fought in the

Above: Hitler enters Sudetenland at Wildenau in 1938.
Left: Henrich Himmler who was Hitler's chief of police and head of the SS.

Nazi Germany skillfully promoted the 1936 Berlin Olympics with colourful posters and magazine spreads. Athletic imagery drew a link between Nazi Germany and ancient Greece. These portrayals symbolized the Nazi racial myth that superior German civilization was the rightful heir of an 'Aryan' culture of classical antiquity.

war or whose families had fought. 'If they were worthy of fighting for Germany and bleeding for Germany, then they must also be considered worthy of continuing to serve the Fatherland in their professions.' It was not until after Hindenburg's death, and Hitler's assumption of his office, combining it with the Reich's Chancellorship and assuming the title of 'Der Führer', that he was able to complete the removal of Jews from public office. In the meantime there were a series of decrees intended to separate Jews from non-Jews in most activities: Jews were not allowed to play non-Jewish music, Jewish children were to be kept distinct in school (and eventually to be confined to their own schools), and the services of Jewish professionals were only to be used by other Jews. The full impact of these and similar measures were felt only by degrees, so that many, both in Germany and outside it, would not necessarily be aware of their full implications. German Jewish organisations

Anti-semitic signs in Germany.
Above right says 'Hyenas are
never decent, neither are Jews.
Jews clear out!'
Right: The sign outside the
village of Oberstdorf says
'Jews not wanted here.'
Above: The sign on the bridge
across the river states: 'The Jew
is our misfortune. Keep him at
arms length.'

Above: From left to right: Hitler, Goebbels wife, Magda, who was bought up in a Jewish household and Goebbels, who was Minister of Propaganda and a fervent anti-semite.

Anti-Semitic propaganda.

Jewish man in Holland being forced to wear the yellow star.

Nazi beer mat, with the wording 'Whoever buys from Jews is a traitor to the people.'

Above: Book-burning in Germany.
Right: Hitler making a speech.

adapted to changing conditions – they had little real alternative – and it was much easier to stay in Germany than to leave it. Currency restrictions by the German government and the marked reluctance expressed by many other countries to accept German-Jewish refugees kept many Jews inside the Reich, and there was perhaps a vague hope that conditions might somehow or other improve; at least, they could not get worse.

Any such feeling was shown up as illusory in the summer and autumn of 1935. The Finance ministry made it clear that while there were strong objections against individual operations directed against Jews there was not the same objection to the gradual elimination of the Jews from the economy by state legislation, while the Party meeting in Nuremberg on 15th September enacted laws on German Citizenship and 'For the Protection of German Blood and Honour' which made clear that Jews were no longer to be regarded as part of the German state. In effect, the Nuremberg Laws, and the various regulations which over the

Jews being forced to clean the streets in Vienna 1938.

Above: Nazis forcibly cutting a Jewish mans hair.

Opposite page: President, Field Marshall Otto von Hindenburg, objected to the exclusion of those who had either fought in the war themselves or whose families had fought. 'If they were worthy of fighting for Germany and bleeding for Germany, then they must also be considered worthy of continuing to serve the Fatherland in their professions.' This poster issued by the German Jewish ex-servicemen's association says that 12,000 Jews died fighting for Germany.

AN DIE DEUTSCHEN MÜTTER!

72000 jüdische Soldaten sind für das Vaterland auf dem Felde der Ehre gefallen.

Christliche und jüdische Helden haben gemeinsam gekämpft und ruhen gemeinsam in fremder Erde.

12000 Juden fielen im Kampf!

Blindwütiger Parteihaß macht vor den Gräbern der Toten nicht Halt.

Deutsche Frauen,

duldet nicht, daß die jüdische Mutter in ihrem Schmerz verhöhnt wird.

Reichsbund jüdischer Frontsoldaten E. V.

following years interpreted those laws, put back the clock of Jewish emancipation and undid all the efforts of previous generations to give Jews in Germany full participation in the political, social, and economic structure of the State. Pressure was exerted by many areas in Germany to declare themselves 'Judenrein'; notices were placed outside German towns and villages declaring that 'Jews are not welcome here' while in many public places, if Jews were permitted entrance at all, they were restricted in where they might walk and where they might sit. The regulations also made clear who was to be regarded as a Jew. The definition depended in the first place upon the status of the individual's grandparents; those who had three Jewish grandparents were themselves defined as Jews even if they or their parents had never been practising Jews – i.e. had become converts. Thus there were many who had never realised that they had any Jewish connections at all until they fell into this category. Care was taken also to categorise all those of mixed ancestry into one or other grade of Mischling.

In 1938 there came a further series of drastic restrictions upon Jews in Germany. The murder of a German diplomat in Paris was seized upon as the excuse for a series of physical attacks upon Jews and Jewish property – Krystall Nacht – and the imposition of an enormous collective fine upon the Jewish community. A series of decrees made it impossible for Jews to

maintain anything that could be considered a 'normal' life in Germany; they could not follow a profession, they could not own a business or any property, and they could not act in any management capacity. As Göring remarked after the meeting which made these decisions, 'I would not want to be a Jew in Germany'. The outbreak of the war led to further restrictions, especially in terms of access to food rations or clothing. After 1941 many Jews were 'resettled' in the East, virtually the only ones left being those who were 'protected' by marriage to a non-Jew or who had managed to go into hiding.

While there were other groups of socially undesirables in Germany – homosexuals, Jehovah's Witnesses, and the half-castes resulting from the stationing in Germany of French colonial soldiers – the only other racially defined group affected by Nazi legislation were the Gypsies. They had for many years before the Nazi accession to power been subjected to discrimination. Attempts had been made to force them to settle in specific locations, but even then they were never regarded as full citizens and eventually they found themselves 'resettled'. Of the other groups, homosexuals were subjected to punishment if they were in any way practising while Jehovah's Witnesses were left untouched if they were prepared to disown their convictions. Those who contravened these guidelines were punished, even being sent to the camps in the East, but unlike the Jews and the Gypsies they were not necessarily singled out for eventual murder.

The issue which remains unclear and debatable is the extent to which this was acquiesced in by 'ordinary' Germans. It has been argued that even where Germans were not enthusiastic about these policies they certainly did not object to them; that even where what was at stake was not the fate of an amorphous mass of unknown people but of known individuals 'ordinary' Germans were not prepared to object. There does however remain a mass of anecdotal evidence that many individuals, however cowed they might have been, did in fact go out of their way in numerous, small ways made to make their own reactions felt.

In the mass this made in practice little difference, but there remains enough to discount a blanket condemnation of all Germans as mass murderers and willing executioners.

Overleaf: Synagogue burning after 'Krystallnacht'.

33

Reich Minister for Public Enlightenment and Propaganda, Joseph Goebbels, delivers a speech during the book burning on the Opernplatz in Berlin 10 May, 1933, Berlin, Germany.

Above and Left: Anti-semitic cartoons published in Dr. Kurt Plischke's 'Der Jude als Rassenschaender: Eine Anklage gegen Juda und eine Mahnung an die deutschen Frauen und Maedchen' (The Jew as Race Defiler: An Accusation against Judah and a Warning to German Women and Girls). Germany, Circa 1935.

Herschel Grynszpan, a Jewish teenager whose parents, along with 17,000 other Polish Jews, had been recently expelled from the Reich, assassinated a German diplomat in Paris, Ernst vom Rath. This gave the Nazis the pretext for 'Krystallnacht'.

On the morning after Kristallnacht local residents watch as the Ober-Ramstadt synagogue is destroyed by fire. The local fire department prevented the fire from spreading to a nearby home, but did not try to limit the damage to the synagogue.

The youth who took the series of photographs of the burning synagogue in Ober-Ramstadt, Georg Schmidt, came from a family that opposed the Nazis. The film was confiscated by police from Schmidt's home the same day the photos were taken, and developed immediately. The prints and negatives were stored in the city hall until a policeman in the service of the American occupation found them and removed them. The son-in-law of the policeman found them in a toolbox and donated them to the city archive. Date: Nov 10, 1938

On the morning after Kristallnacht local residents watch as the Ober-Ramstadt synagogue is destroyed by fire.

Jews arrested during Kristallnacht line up for roll call at the Buchenwald concentration camp. November 1938.

On November 9, 1938, the Nazis unleashed a wave of pogroms against Germany's Jews. In the space of a few hours, thousands of synagogues and Jewish businesses and homes were damaged or destroyed. This event came to be called Kristallnacht ('Night of Broken Glass') for the shattered store windowpanes that carpeted German streets.

The pretext for this violence was the assassination of Ernst vom Rath by Herschel Grynszpan. Though portrayed as spontaneous outbursts of popular outrage, these pogroms were calculated acts of retaliation carried out by the SA, SS, and local Nazi party organizations.

Germans marching in Poland in 1939.

The Nazi War against the Allies

THE WAR BETWEEN Germany and the Franco-British alliance opened in September 1939 with a German attack on Poland; an intervention by the Russians, attacking into the east of Poland, led rapidly to the destruction of the Polish army and the division of the state between German and Russian occupied areas. A period of a so-called 'phoney war' was followed in the spring of 1940 by the German Army firstly over-running Denmark and conquering Norway and secondly attacking the Allied armies in the West, leading to the occupation of the Netherlands, Luxembourg, and Belgium and the surrender of the French army and the division of France between occupied and unoccupied zones. Meanwhile the Italians had entered the war, occupying parts of Southern France and eventually launching an attack upon Greece.

Now standing alone against the Germans and Italians, Britain continued the war in the air and succeeded in averting a possible invasion. Unable to bring the war to an end in the west the Germans concentrated on the East, building up alliances against the Russians. A failed attempt to buy off Yugoslavia led to an invasion of that country by the Germans, Hungarians, and Bulgarians. After its defeat it was divided between a puppet state of Croatia, an occupied Serbia, and the transfer of various other territories to Bulgaria. Assistance to the Italians in Greece led to the defeat of that country and its partition amongst the Italians, Germans, and the Bulgarians. That venture into the Balkans was followed by a delayed attack on Russia in which Germany was assisted by the armies of the 'allied' states of Hungary and Rumania.

The fluctuating fortunes of the war on the Eastern front had led by the autumn of 1942 to what was to be the furthest limit of German territorial power in Europe. But the entry of the United States into the war and the failure of the Germans to destroy the Russians implied also that the Reich could no longer contemplate an extra-European future for European Jews. It was however as a consequence of the indecisive war against the Russians that the parallel war being waged by the Reich, its war against the Jews, reached its decisive stage.

Above: Molotov signs the Soviet / Nazi non-aggression pact, August 1939. Ribbentrop, the German representative stands behind Molotov Joseph Stalin stands on his left.

Right: Hitler poses for a propaganda film in Paris, after France's captulation in 1940.

The War Against The Jews

THE PROGRESS OF the German army between 1939 and the summer of 1941 had brought the Jewish communities of Norway, Denmark, Holland, Belgium and France under German rule. In some countries the rule was direct, whereas in others some form of puppet administration was established. Denmark had been over-run so quickly that there had been no for-mal state of war, and the Germans left the administration there under a form of Protectorate, the Jews remaining under the protection of the King and Government. Some countries were German allies or satellites, and there conditions for the Jews varied greatly. In Italy and Hungary for example Jews were in effect protected by the Government so long as an independent government existed, and where the Italian Army was the 'occupying power', as in the south of France, Greece, or parts of Croatia, the Jews were also in practice protected. When however the Germans finally took over in Italy and in Hungary Jews were subjected to the full programme of deportation and extermination.

The pattern was fairly constant. The first steps were to create a feeling of isolation for the Jews and to separate them from the non-Jewish communities among whom they had been living. They were forced into Jewish neighbourhoods – something approaching the ghettos that were being established in Eastern Europe; individual Jews were forced to wear a yellow badge of some sort labelling them as Jews and marking them out from the body of the occupied territories; and the Jews were denied access to the normal features of life, such as shopping for food. Jews who could be claimed as having been of German origin were considered as falling directly under German control and therefore as liable for deportation, and even in those countries where there was a semblance of local autonomy pressure was put on the local government to surrender Jews for deportation.

It was during the summer of 1941 that there seems to have developed an overall plan designed to 'deal' with the Jews of Europe. The head of the SS responsible for Jewish affairs, Reinhard Heydrich, secured formal approval from Göring to prepare such plans which were being developed in the autumn. A conference of executive heads was held at Wannsee in January 1942 at which Heydrich and Eichmann informed their colleagues of the decision to drop all ideas of 'emigration' and to replace them by the concept of 'resettlement in the

East'. They drew up lists of the Jews to be deported to the East as a first step in the final solution; the minutes of the conference note that 'Europe is to be combed through from West to East.' Transit ghettos were to be established, and from them Jews were to be transferred further. By the end of 1942 the process of the extermination of the Jews in Poland was in full swing, and the deportations from France, Belgium, and Holland had begun. In Norway the local government under Quisling participated actively, even though some of the Norwegian Jews were able to escape to Sweden. In some of the countries of Western Europe groups of gentiles did their best to assist Jews to evade this round-up, but for the most part there was little chance of escape. Even so, a pattern began to appear. In France or in Belgium there were different survival rates between Jews who had entered the country in the period after the First World War and those who had been longer

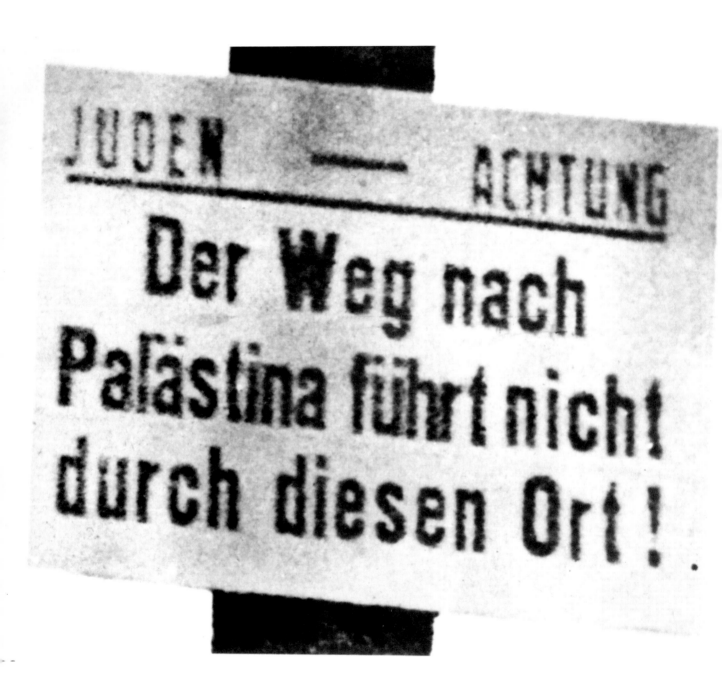

Sign outside a German village. It says 'Jews. Attention. The road to Palestine
does not go through this locality'.

established and who had in some sense come to be recognised as 'our' Jews.

The outstanding example of a community of Jews that was saved as a result of the actions of the non-Jews amongst whom they lived was that of Denmark. There are a number of misconceptions about the part played by the Danes, such as whether or not the King of Denmark actually wore a Yellow Star or merely threatened that if such an order was introduced he himself would also wear it. Equally there has been argument amongst historians as to how the details of the projected round-up of the Danish Jews fell into the hands of the leading members of the Danish government, and the extent to which various elements of the German occupying forces might have acquiesced in the transfer of the bulk of Danish Jews to Sweden. The fact remains that the overwhelming majority of Danish Jews escaped, and those few who were captured by the Germans were sent not to a death camp but to Terezin where they remained under the watchful eye of the Danish government until their final release.

In Eastern and South-Eastern Europe the story became more complicated. The attack by the Germans on Yugoslavia and the overrunning of the Balkan peninsula led to the creation of a satellite state of Croatia as well as the occupation of the rest of Serbia by the German armies. The German army in Serbia played a leading role in the destruction of the Jewish communities there, while the Croats were not backward in attacking any one who was not a Roman Catholic Croat. The Italian army did its best to smuggle as many Jews as possible into Italy or various camps on the Adriatic islands under Italian control. When Germany attacked Russia the Hungarians and the Rumanians joined in the war. The Rumanians displayed a particular ferocity against the Jews of Rumania itself and of those parts of Russia which came under their control. At times even the Germans expressed some concern at the untidiness of the Rumanians and their failure to bury their victims. Many Rumanian Jews were transferred to erstwhile Russian territory, but one segment was left untouched. There had been for many generations Rumanian Jews in Wallachia – the heartland of the old Principality – and these had in many ways integrated into Rumanian life. Some had close personal connections with Governmental leaders, and as a consequence a nucleus of Rumanian Jews survived. The Churches there also played a part by issuing bogus baptismal certificates and thus protecting a considerable number of these long-term Jewish residents. And while the Rumanian Government was undoubtedly guilty of appalling atrocities inside Rumania it did not hand over any Jews for death in Auschwitz.

The Bulgarians were equally ambivalent in their treatment of Jews. Bulgaria had allied itself to Germany in the attacks on Yugoslavia and Greece and as a reward various territories in Macedonia and Thrace were transferred to Bulgarian rule. When pressure was put upon the Bulgarian government it had no problem about transferring Jews from these territories to

Right: Anne Frank, October 10, 1942, just a few months after she went into hiding with her family in Amsterdam. Anne was 13 years old at the time. Born in Frankfurt, Germany on June 12, 1929, the Frank family moved to Amsterdam after the Nazis appropriated power in 1933. They led a quiet life until the German invasion of the Netherlands in 1940. As a result of ever-increasing anti-Jewish measures and mounting uncertainty for their safety, the family went into hiding in July 1942, She and her family stayed in hiding until they were betrayed; she died of typhus in Bergen-Belsen in March 1945. Anne's father, Otto Frank, survived the war. Anne kept several diaries during her stay in the Secret Annex. In them she described life in the Annex, her dreams, and her fears. These diaries survived the war, and the first version, edited by Otto Frank, was published by a Dutch publishing house. They have been translated in 50 languages and have sold almost 20 million copies worldwide.

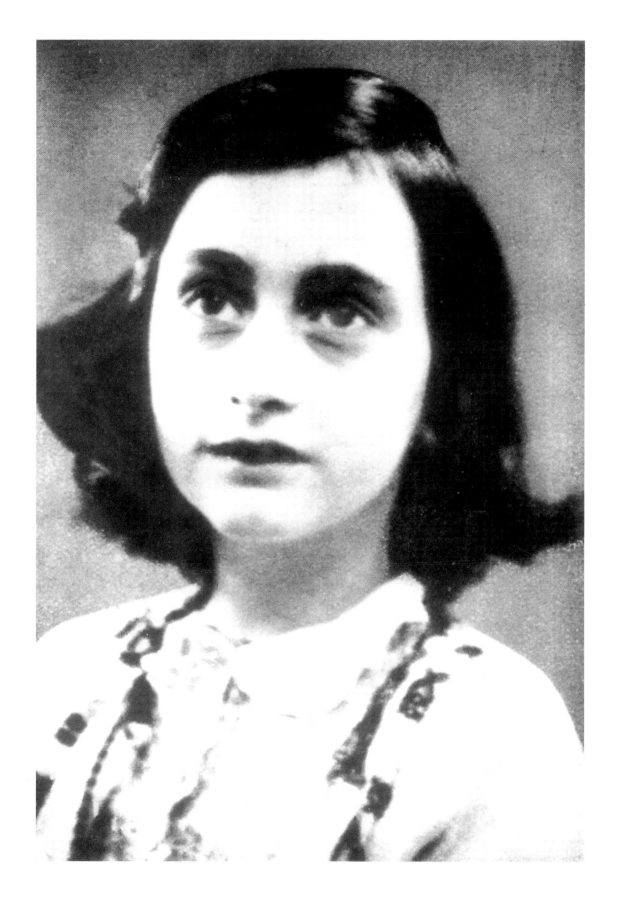

Auschwitz. It refused however to transfer its 'own' Jews to German control, and in consequence the Bulgarian Jewish community largely survived.

Greek Jews were originally protected by the Italian army, but when in 1943 the Italians 'changed sides' the Germans took over control and were very active in uncovering small Jewish communities, even in the small islands off the European mainland. Many Jews in the Balkans were however of Spanish origin, descendants of the Jews expelled from Spain and Portugal at the end of the fifteenth century, and in many cases local Spanish and Portuguese consular officials attempted to give protection, claiming them as basically Spanish or Portuguese subjects. The Germans were punctilious in recognising these claims, having always

accepted that 'foreigners' were not normally to be touched by their plans.

Jews in Slovakia and Hungary were equally to be in a unique position. The puppet government established in Slovakia was headed by Father Tiszo, a Roman Catholic priest, who was an ardent anti-semite. Persecution of the Jews proceeded apace, but deportations to Auschwitz were for some time halted by an attempt to 'buy' the Jews of Slovakia. In Hungary Jews had for long been recognised citizens of the Hungarian state, and even though the head of government, Admiral Horthy, had introduced programmes of discrimination they had not lost all their rights. One of the most significant of these had been the continuing liability for military service. Even after Hungary had entered the war

Right: Young jewish girl after she has been attacked by a Ukrainian mob.
Overleaf: Jewish man being attacked in Poland.

against Russia Jews were still conscripted,
for labour battalions, and the Hungarian
army was not prepared at that stage to see
action taken against them. Their lives were
left relatively untouched, so that a time
when virtually all the other Jewish
communities had suffered devastation these
communities were living in a virtual
cocoon.

Right: Jewish women awaiting execution.

Above: A German police officer shoots Jewish women still alive after a mass execution of Jews from the Mizocz ghetto.

Left: German soldiers of the Waffen-SS and the Reich Labor Service look on as a member of an Einsatzgruppe prepares to shoot a Ukrainian Jew kneeling on the edge of a mass grave filled with corpses. Date: 1941 - 1943

Above: Portrait of Reinhard Heydrich seated at his desk.

Reinhard Heydrich (1904-1942) was head of the Nazi Security Police (Sicherheitspolizei, SIPO), the Security service (Sicherheitsdienst, SD), and later the Reich Security Main Office (Reichssicheitshauptamt, RSHA). In these capacities he had unlimited control over the fate of those deemed enemies of the Reich. From 1939 he was also chief executor of Nazi anti-Jewish policy. It was Heydrich who was in charge of the Einsatzgruppen and it was he who convened the Wannsee conference of Jan 1942, to discuss the program of the final solution. Late in 1941 Heydrich was appointed governor of the Protectorate of Bohemia and Moravia. Six months later he was assassinated by Czech resistance fighters in an ambush near Prague.

A group of Jewish women and girls huddle together on a beach near Liepaja prior to their execution by Latvian SD and police. In the background other Jews are being forced to undress by Latvian police.

Above: A group of naked Jewish women and girls walk to the execution site on the beach near Liepaja. In the background other Jews are being forced to undress by Latvian police.

Left: A Latvian policeman leads a group of Jewish women to the execution site on the beach near Liepaja.

This series of photographs depicts a killing action perpetrated against the Jews of Liepaja on 15-17 December, 1941. The three-day action, in which over half the Jewish community was killed, took place in the village of Skede, 15km. north of Liepaja, on the site of a former military training grounds in the dunes overlooking the Baltic Sea. On the night of December 13, Latvian police began rounding up Jews of all ages in Liepaja. They were brought to the women's prison, where they were crowded into a courtyard that was not large enough to contain them all. The next evening and following morning, December 14-15, the Jews were transported to the Skede military training grounds, where they were assembled in a wooden barn. In groups of twenty, the Jews were led to the dunes, where a long ditch had been dug that ran parallel to the shore. At a point fifty meters from the ditch, the Jews were instructed to lie face down on the ground. Half of them were then told to get up and strip down to their underwear. The clothes were piled in heaps, which were later removed by German military trucks. Once undressed, the Jews were marched to the ditches, where they were told to remove the remainder of their clothing. The victims were then positioned along the ditch facing the sea so that their bodies would tumble into the trench as they were shot. For the corpses that did not fall in by themselves, there was a

'kicker' who pushed them in. The mass shootings were carried out by members of a Latvian SD guard platoon, units of the 21st Latvian police battalion and members of the Schutzpolizei-Dienstabteilung [German security police] under the command of the local SS and Police Leader Fritz Dietrich. An entry from the wartime diary of Fritz Dietrich puts the number of Jews killed in the action at 2,746, while records from the SIPO office in Liepaja offer the figure of 2,731. A SIPO report notes that the entire action was filmed by the Germans to show that it was carried out primarily by Latvian security forces. Two German members of the SD, one of them identified as SS Oberscharführer Carl Strott, took a series of still photographs with a Minox subminiature camera. It is reported that Strott, whip in hand, forced groups of Jews to pose for him during the action. These photographs were preserved through the efforts of a Latvian Jew named David Zivcon, who worked as an electrician in the offices of the SD in Liepaja. Some weeks or months after the action in Skede, Zivcon was told to repair the electrical wiring in Strott's apartment. No one else was present while Zivcon worked. In a half-open drawer he noticed four rolls of film which he examined and recognized as a massacre of Liepajan Jews. Zivcon smuggled them out, got a friend

Liepajan Jewish women awaiting execution.

to make copies and then returned the originals by faking a power failure as a pretext for reentering Strott's apartment. Zivcon then placed the photo prints in a metal box and buried them in a horse stable. After the liberation he retrieved the photographs and turned them over to Soviet military intelligence. These pictures were subsequently put into evidence at the Nuremberg War Crimes Trials.

Above: SS officer kicks prisoners into a truck.

Above: A Latvian policeman walks along the edge of a mass grave towards the bodies Jewish women and children who have just been executed.

Known as a 'kicker,' it was his job to push the bodies into the mass grave that did not fall in during the shooting. This was necessary to make room on the edge of the grave for the next group of Jews to be shot.

Portrait of Adolf Eichmann, 1940, Germany.

SS-Obersturmbannfuehrer Karl Adolf Eichmann (1906-1962) was head of the Department for Jewish Affairs in the Gestapo from 1941 to 1945 and was chief of operations in the deportation of three million Jews to extermination camps. He joined the Austrian Nazi party in 1932 and later became a member of the SS. In 1934 he served as an SS corporal in the Dachau concentration camp. That same year he joined the SD and attracted the attention of Heinrich Himmler and Reinhard Heydrich. By 1935

Eichmann was already working in the Jewish section, where he was investigating possible 'solutions to the Jewish question.' He was even sent to Palestine to discuss the viability of large scale immigration to the Middle East with Arab leaders. British authorities, however, forced him to leave. With the takeover of Austria in March 1938, Eichmann was sent to Vienna to promote Jewish emigration. He set up the Zentralstelle fuer juedische Auswanderung [Centre for Jewish Emigration], which was so successful that similar offices were soon established in Prague and Berlin. In 1939 Eichmann returned to Berlin, where he assumed the directorship of Section IV B4, Jewish affairs and evacuation, in the Reich Security Main Office. It was Eichmann who organized the Wannsee Conference of January 1942, which focused on issues related to the 'final solution of the Jewish question.' From this point Eichmann assumed the leading role in the deportation of European Jews to the death camps, as well as in the plunder of their property. At the end of the war, Eichmann was arrested and confined to an American internment camp, but he was able to escape unrecognized. He fled to Argentina and lived under the assumed name of Ricardo Klement for ten years until Israeli Mossad agents abducted him in 1960 to stand trial in Jerusalem. The controversial and highly publicized trial lasted from April 2 to August 14, 1961. Eichmann was sentenced to death and executed in Ramleh Prison on May 31, 1962.

Concentration Camps

ONE OF THE MOST misunderstood aspects of the Nazi system was the structure of concentration camps. Largely run by the SS they differed widely. Some, such as Dachau, were designed to be re-educational institutions for those who were politically unreliable. Some, such as Matthausen, were work-camps, where people were worked hard, even to death, without being necessarily intended to be killed. Some were intended to be wholly 'factories of death', such as Belzec, Chelmno, Treblinka or Sobibor. Some of these camps were run by the Economic and Administrative Main Office of the SS and designed to be part of an SS dominated factory system. Best known, of course, were Auschwitz and Majdanek, where millions were put to death. Even these

however were partially linked to work centres and indeed were themselves the centres of a wide circle of sub-camps, some so small as to be no more than the work-force attached to a single factory. Thus many were sent to Auschwitz, almost immediately to be used in one or other of these sub-camps or in Auschwitz Three (Monowitz where there was a big chemical complex) there to be worked until they were no longer fit for labour, and then to be brought back to the main camp for 'disposal'.

The initial camps, such as Dachau, were intended for political prisoners and for harsh re-education of dissidents. But by 1938 their purpose was being extended and immediately after Krystallnacht they were a part of the process of removing Jews from German life. It was in the late summer and autumn of 1941 that they were developed as part of the process of physical destruction of the Jews of Europe as well as other elements considered unsuitable for Hitler's concept of German rule in Europe. Plans were laid down for the creation of the camps that were solely 'death factories', such as Belzec where there was the first use of gas chambers, and for the development of a major set of camps at Auschwitz where Soviet Prisoners of War were used to check the efficiency of the gassing process. These camps came under the jurisdiction of the SS, but many of those involved in the various procedures were drawn from various nationalities in Eastern Europe. Indeed, many of the day-to-day details of the life and administration of the camps were in the hands of 'trusties', the so-called 'kapos', who were given various privileges in return for their services. In many cases,

however, the alternative to acceptance of these privileges was an early despatch to the gas chambers.

There was no uniformity in these camps, even in those devoted completely to the production of death. The deliberate and systematic destruction of European Jewry began in the early summer of 1942. In each of the ghettos of Poland the overwhelming majority of the Jews were marshalled and transported to a camp selected by the SS organisation at either a national or local level. Sometimes the removal of the local population was virtually total and in other places a process of selection was gone through. Where there was selection the local Judenrat was made responsible for the choice. The movement was usually by train, and indeed the whole process was dependent upon the efficient use of the railway system. Trains were hired by the SS, and elaborate accounting procedures were created

The entrance to Trzebinia work camp.

Above: Reichsfuehrer SS Heinrich Himmler shakes the hand of an SS officer during a tour of the Monowitz-Buna building site, Auschwitz-Monowitz, 17 July, 1942 - 18 July, 1942.

Overleaf: Newly arrived women camp inmates with shaved heads. Those selected for slave labour would have been compelled to wear a stripped uniform. The rest would have been murdered.

to ensure that the railway authorities received their rent and sent out receipts. Once the trains had arrived at their destinations the Jews and their possessions were separated; the Jews might again go through some process of selection so that a number of the fittest could be reserved for processing the victims. But thereafter the remainder were shepherded to areas for undressing prior to them being given 'showers'. It was at that stage that the majority began to realise their fate. Some had done so earlier, and there were to be incidents when the victims turned upon the guards on duty at the railway sidings. At times they were able to seize their weapons and shoot at the guards before themselves being shot down by the rest. After gassing had finished it was left to the Jewish special groups – the Sonderkommandos – to drag the corpses from the gas chambers, search them for valuables, deposit the bodies in the furnaces or on the funeral pyres, and then later clear away the ashes for the next

group. Others would have the task of going through the possessions of those thus murdered and sorting them into appropriate categories. Those forming the Sonderkommandos had themselves but a short extension of life and all too frequently they themselves were consigned to the gas chambers to be replaced by others in their turn. Treblinka, Chelmno, Belzec, and Sobibor operated largely in 1942 and 1943 so that by the time of the last great destruction of Polish Jews, the so-called 'Erntefest' (harvest festival), the Jewish population of Poland had been virtually destroyed. In some of these camps there is knowledge of episodes of resistance, the classic case being the great revolt in Sobibor which resulted in the decision to close the camp down earlier than intended; in others there is little or no evidence since there were few if any survivors. Of the hundreds of thousands who for instance went through Belzec only two survived, and the camp itself was so effectively dismantled

Above: Bales of human hair ready for shipment to Germany found in one of the Auschwitz warehouses when the camp was liberated. In Auschwitz 7,000 kilos of human hair was found at liberation. Date: Jan 1945

Left: Baskets woven from the hair of Nazi victims.

View of the entrance to the main camp of Auschwitz-Birkenau.

that it is only possible to discover its extent and the number of its victims by the methods of classical archaeology.

Better known of course was Auschwitz, situated where the North/South and West/East railways systems of Europe crossed. It soon became the focal point for the receipt of the masses of Jews from outside Poland destined for murder. At the same time however the availability of a cheap and unending source of labour was attractive both to the SS leaders themselves and also to various German industrialists.

Hence was established as part of the general Auschwitz complex Auschwitz III, the Buna rubber factories at Monowitz. The process of selection at Auschwitz thus became more complex. Those who had a 'trade' or who looked healthy could be selected for the various work programmes either within the main camps themselves or the smaller sub-camps associated with Auschwitz. There too could be selected those required by the infamous Mengele for his so-called 'experiments'. The others, all unwanted, could thereafter be consigned directly to the gas chambers. The camp was

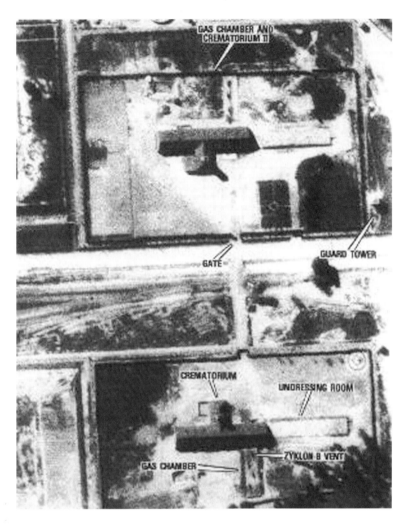

This U.S. Army Airforce aerial photograph showing the gas chambers and crematoria 2 and 3 at the Auschwitz-Birkenau (Auschwitz II) extermination camp. Auschwitz, Poland, August 25, 1944. Those who had been selected to die were led to gas chambers. In order to prevent panic, camp guards told the victims that they were going to take showers to rid themselves of lice. The guards instructed them to turn over all their valuables and to undress. Then they were driven naked into the 'showers.' A guard closed and locked the steel door. In some killing centres, carbon monoxide was piped into the chamber. In others, camp guards threw 'Zyklon B' pellets down an air shaft. Zyklon B was a highly poisonous insecticide also used to kill rats and insects.

well organised and efficient; if for example there were initially too few furnaces invitations to tender were sent to the leading manufacturers in Germany, and the firm of Topfe Und Sohne were proud to display their metal plate on the installed products and to send its engineers to service them. If on occasion the ash still contained fragments of bone then enquiries could be made as to the availability of bone-crushing machinery. Sometimes accidents did happen; there was one consignment of extremely fit Greek Jews sent to Auschwitz intended for labouring

Above: One of many warehouses at Auschwitz in which the Germans stored clothing belonging to victims of the camp. This photograph was taken after the liberation of the camp. Auschwitz, Poland, after January 1945.

purposes who were mistakenly despatched immediately on arrival to the gas chambers. Broadly speaking however those who were transported there were punctiliously asked whether they had a trade, and those who did make such an avowal were spared – even if it were only for a moment. Thus survived the chemist Primo Levi and the young Hugo Grynn.

The facilities at Auschwitz were greatly enlarged during the time when it was in service. Probably the biggest enlargement was during the winter of 1943/44, when the railway sidings were extended from outside Auschwitz I to the interior of Auschwitz II, Birkenau. The classic image of Auschwitz/Birkenau - the great archway through which ran the railway line into the sidings beyond - was the result of this enlargement and was the warning to some of the inmates, especially Rudolf Vrba, that the destruction of the last surviving Jewish community, the Hungarian Jews, was at hand. The complex of camps was to become the symbol of the Holocaust, and to become the largest Jewish cemetery in Europe.

Life in Auschwitz, as in most other camps, was unspeakably harsh. Even those that were primarily 'work camps' produced inhuman conditions. The SS themselves estimated that the 'normal' stay in these conditions would be no more than three months. Where labour was cheap and apparently inexhaustible no care needed to be taken for the safety of the workers. In the quarries of Matthausen or in the rocket factories at Peenemunde the death roll was huge. The incessant roll-calls, the grossly inadequate rations, the continual pressure from all sides made life pure hell. The often senseless brutality of the guards led many in despair to break the regulations in order to court death. Only an intense will to survive in order to bear witness kept some

Top: Majdanek Camp. Below: Murder operations using poison gas began at Majdanek in October 1942 and continued until the end of 1943. Majdanek had three gas chambers located in one building, which used both carbon monoxide and Zyklon B gas to kill prisoners. 1941-44

Above: Corpses of women piled up on the floor of Block 11. Auschwitz, February 1945.

Right: Survivors queuing up for rations provided by the British Army.

Bergen-Belsen, near Hanover in northwest Germany, was established in March 1943 as a special camp for prominent Jews of belligerent and neutral states, who might be exchanged for German citizens interned abroad. Conditions in the camp were originally good by concentration camp standards, and most prisoners were not subjected to forced labour. However, by April 1945 over 60,000 prisoners were incarcerated in Belsen in two camps located 1.5 miles apart. Members of the British Royal Artillery 63rd Anti-Tank Regiment liberated Belsen on April 15 and arrested its commandant, Josef Kramer. Between April 18 and April 28, the dead were buried. At first the SS guards were made to collect and bury the bodies, but eventually the British had to resort to bulldozers to push the thousands of bodies into mass graves.

of the inmates alive, and many of those who survived paid tribute to the others whose friendship kept them able to continue.

Ironically, the image which most in the western world have in mind in relation to these camps was the most untypical of them all, Belsen and Dachau. The advance of the Allied armies in the spring of 1945 and their uncovering of the appalling conditions in these camps led to their image as being typical of all. Belsen, liberated by the British, with its tens of thousands of dead and near dead lying around was not the result of the death camp system. Rather it was originally intended as a camp for 'prominent' prisoners due for exchange. It was only in the last months of the Reich, when the German armies were retreating from the Russians and the SS attempted to evacuate the inmates from the East that the inmates, marched or otherwise transferred to the west, were dumped into these camps. The breakdown of all administration, accompanied by the criminal neglect of the camp administrators, led to the conditions which greeted the Allies and the war correspondents.

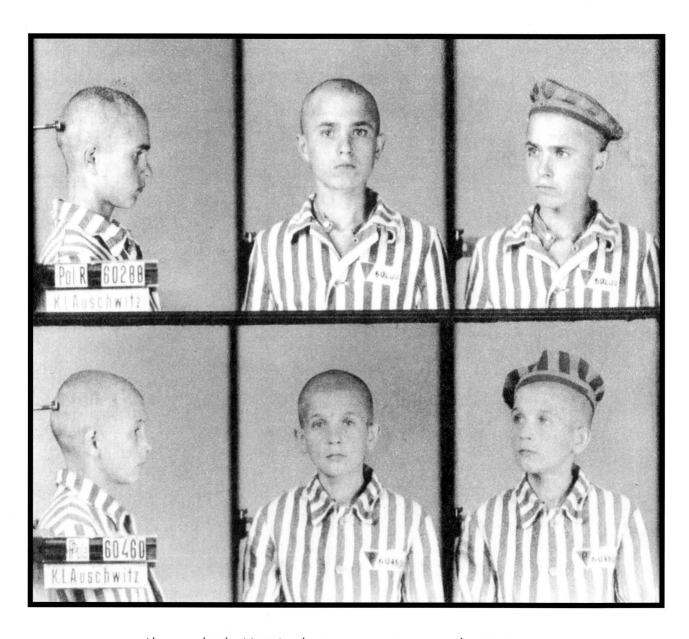

Above and right: Nazi Auschwitz concentration camp identity pictures.

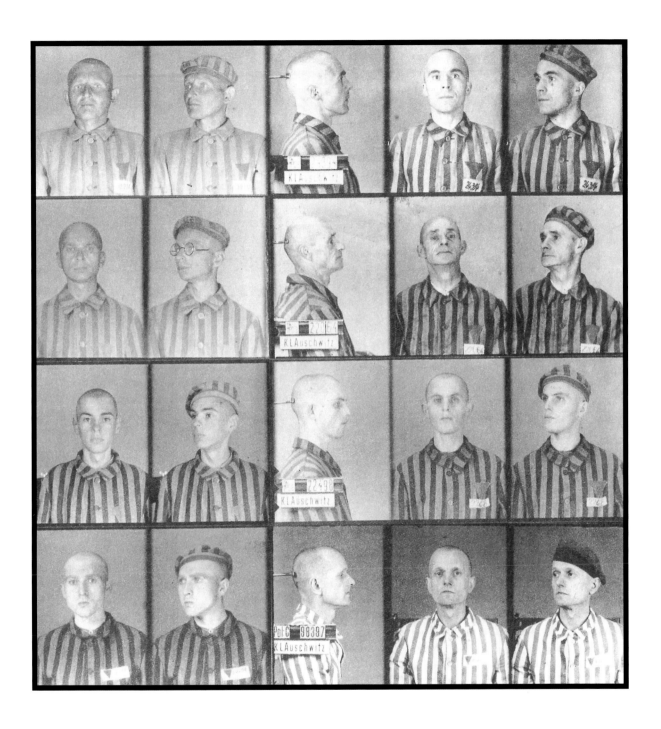

Dr Mengele. Between 1939 and 1945, at least seventy medical research projects involving cruel and often lethal experimentation on human subjects were conducted in Nazi concentration camps. These projects were carried out by established institutions within the Third Reich and fell into three areas: research aimed at improving the survival and rescue of German troops; testing of medical procedures and pharmaceuticals; and experiments that sought to confirm Nazi racial ideology. More than seven thousand victims of such medical experiments have been documented. Victims include Jews, Poles, Roma (Gypsies), political prisoners, Soviet prisoners of war, homosexuals, and Catholic priests.

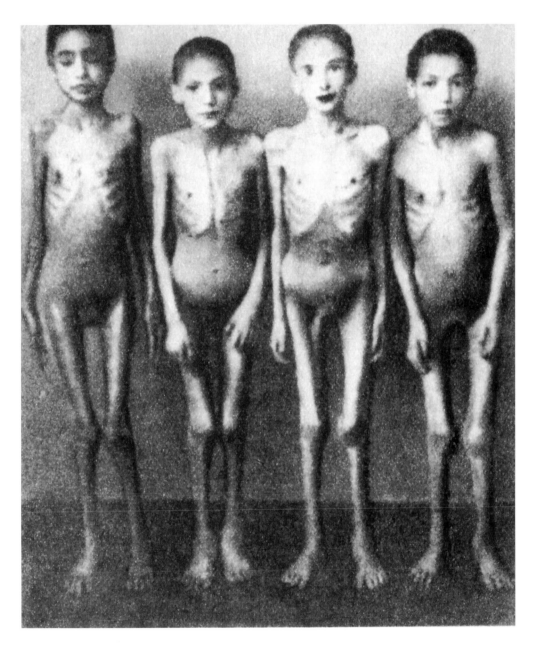

Above and following page Children who had experiments conducted on them by Dr Mengele and others.

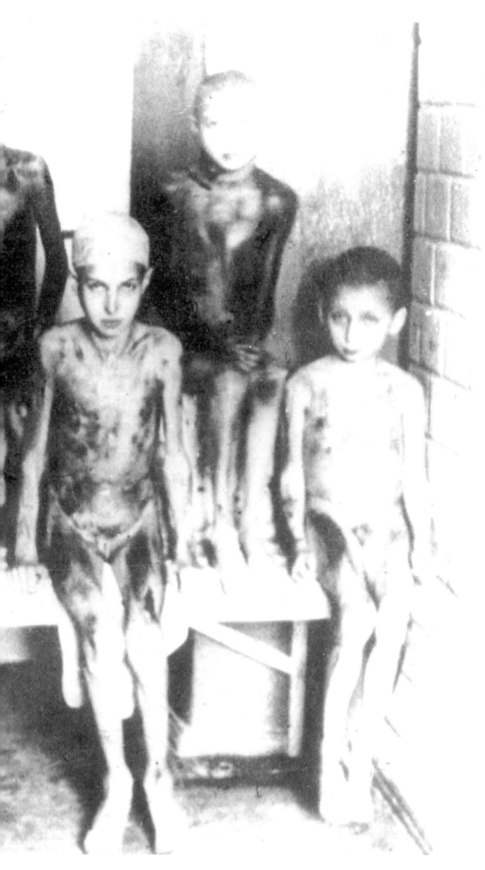

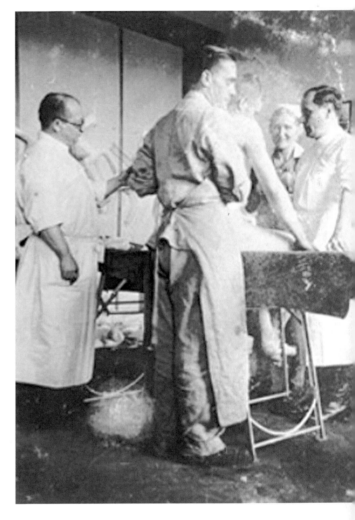

Above: Dr Carl Clauberg

Dr. Carl Clauberg (left) with his staff in the operating room in Block 10, Auschwitz. Dr. Clauberg experimented with non-surgical methods of sterilization on Jewish female prisoners in Auschwitz I. He was later imprisoned by the Russians for his part in these pseudo-scientific experiments.

Prisoners at Auschwitz.

Camp survivor in Bergen-
Belsen, 1945.

Left: SS officer Eichelsdoerfer, the commandant of the Kaufering IV concentration camp, stands among the corpses of prisoners killed in his camp. 27 April - 30 April, 1945, Belsen.

Overleaf: Jewish women in cattle cars on on their way to death camps.

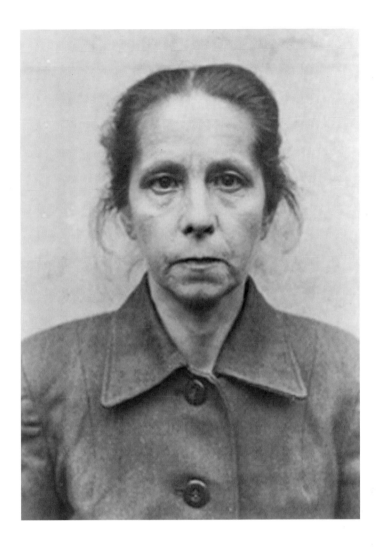

Juana Bormann, part of a series of mug shots taken of former guards and prisoners from the Belsen camp before their trial in front of a British Military Tribunal. One of the oldest SS staff members in Bergen-Belsen at age 52, Juana Bormann had a reputation as a sadist. Witnesses constantly repeated how previously at Auschwitz she would set her dog upon prisoners and watched as they were torn apart. Questions of her sanity arose during the Bergen-Belsen Trial but they were not enough to keep her from being found guilty by the British Military Tribunal. She was sentenced to death and hanged on 13 December 1945 in Hameln, Germany.

Above: American photographs of Nordhausen 13 April 1945.
Opposite top: Survivors at Dachau. Opposite below: American soldiers with victims at Dachau.

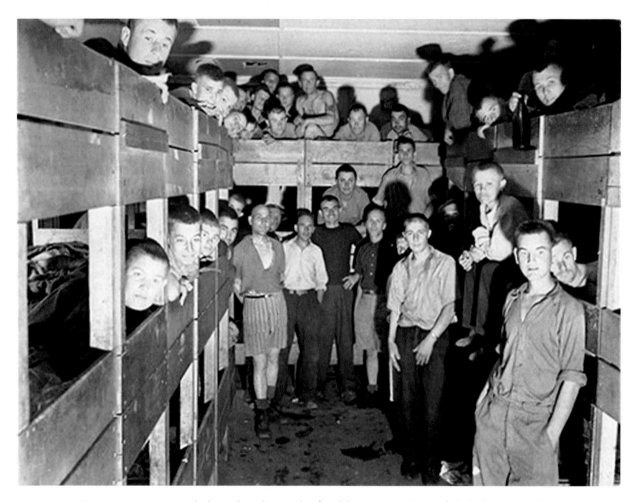

Survivors in a crowded Dachau barrack after liberation. 29 April -15 May , 1945.

Left: American soldiers view the bodies of prisoners shot by the SS during the liberation of the Ohrdruf, a Buchenwald Sub-Camp. April 13, 1945

Above: One of the piles of shoes of camp victims discovered after the liberation of Belzec camp.

Above: Corpses of Auschwitz prisoners in block 11 of the main camp
(Auschwitz I), as discovered by Soviet war crimes investigators

Left: A door to a gas chamber in Auschwitz. The note reads: Harmful gas! Entering endangers your life.
Date: Feb 1945

Left: View of the execution wall next to Block 11 in the Auschwitz I camp after liberation. After Jan 29, 1945

Top: View of the entrance to the main camp of Auschwitz (Auschwitz I). The gate bears the motto 'Arbeit Macht Frei' (Work makes one free).

Below: A sign on the electric fence in Auschwitz. The sign reads:'caution, danger', after January 1945.

Prisoners' orchestra during a Sunday concert for the SS-men in Auschwitz.
The orchestra was probably conducted by the inmate Franciszek Nierychlo.

Above: A survivor in Dachau on the day of liberation 29 April, 1945.

Opposite below: An exhibit of human remains and artifacts retrieved by the U.S. Army from a pathology laboratory run by the SS in Buchenwald. These items were used as evidence of SS atrocities. The items include tattooed skin taken from executed prisoners, a lampshade made of human skin, and two shrunken heads from Polish prisoners who were recaptured after escaping from the camp and executed.

Above: Female prisoners at forced labour in Ravensbrück concentration camp.

Jewish resistance and rescuers

ONE ISSUE FOR the Jews of Europe which emerged almost from the beginning of Nazi rule was how to react. Some in Germany felt, initially, that they should maintain a low profile and that eventually conditions might improve. Some sought to flee the country. Others felt that they should make a virtue out of this new way of life and almost ostentatiously make their Jewishness obvious. 'Wear the Yellow Badge with pride' was the slogan of one, Zionist, newspaper. But as German control spread over Europe, and as it became clearer that they faced a desperate future Jews had to consider what actions they might take. Few could have any control over their actions or their fate. For most of them there was no alternative to obeying the commands of their new masters. Ground down by hunger or brutality they were herded to their deaths in either extermination camps or on hastily designated slaughter grounds.

Much has been written about the extent of 'resistance' to the Nazis and about how many went 'like lambs to the slaughter.' Clearly formal, armed resistance was not easy, and it has been pointed out that there were many non-Jews – e.g. Soviet prisoners of war – who were murdered in their millions. Many of the Jewish men – all of the women and children – had had no military training or access to arms. But resistance was not necessarily to be found in conventional methods, and it has been strongly argued that even the determination to stay alive, to outlive Hitler, was a form of resistance. The desire to ensure that there were records of what had transpired was equally a form of resistance. Nonetheless there were a number of resistance groups formed in the ghettos of Eastern Europe, and in some the Judenrat itself played an important part in them. Best known of these resistance groups were those in Warsaw where the deportation policies of the Germans had reduced the Jewish population in the ghetto from some 300,000 to an official 30,000. In so doing the Germans had in effect made it more possible for the youth movements to organise themselves more effectively as well as to put them into a state of virtual desperation. Having little or no future for themselves they could concentrate on a policy of resistance. Even if the various political factions could not unite sufficiently amongst themselves for a common command group and even if they could not secure adequate support from the various Polish organisations outside the ghetto, their uprising in May 1943 when for several weeks they held off the German attempt to destroy the last of the ghetto made a definite impact upon opinion elsewhere.

There were other occasions of resistance. By their very nature many of them are unknown or unknowable. There are known instances of individual attempts to thwart the processes of selection at the camps when all involved were immediately shot down. There was the break-out from the camp at Sobibor when the arrival of several hundred Russian Jewish prisoners of war gave some organised format and led to the escape of several hundreds of the inmates and to the devastation and enforced closure of the camp. There was the resistance movement in Auschwitz itself which manifested itself both in the deliberate preservation of records of what had happened there amongst the very pits

Young members of the resistance being executed in Minsk, October 1941.
On the left is a 17-year old Jewish girl Marsha Bruskina.

containing the ashes of the victims and in the attempt by the women to destroy one of the great crematoria. In Lithuania resistance showed itself in escapes from the ghettos of Vilna and Kovno to the forests where many were able to join groups of partisans - Russian soldiers cut off from their units but maintaining the war against the Germans. Many of these units became purely Jewish, and some of them were responsible for the protection of the so-called 'family camps' where some of the women and children were able to find shelter. These Jewish partisan groups were eventually to be dissolved by the orders of the Soviet High Command, but many of the survivors, incorporated into standard Russian and Lithuanian Divisions, played a prominent part in such operations as the liberation of Kovno and Vilna.

The issue of specifically Jewish resistance groups was irrelevant in western Europe, for there many prominent Jews, such as Marc Bloch (France) or Primo Levi (Italy), were included in the individual national resistance movements.

The issue of Jewish rescue remains one of the most controversial in the study of the Holocaust. The questions of when did the Allies know what was going on, how much did they know, and what could have been done about this knowledge have been, and are still, hotly debated. British intelligence services, decoding German Enigma messages in the late summer of 1941, undoubtedly were aware of the initial activities of the various Einsatzgruppen on the Eastern front, and although the cessation of these messages closed that channel of communication secret courier services from Poland brought news of the operation of various death camps in the spring of 1942. The famous Reigner telegram of June 1942 revealing the existence of the overall death programme was largely ignored by Allied Governments until

December when Washington, London, and Moscow issued a joint declaration revealing their knowledge of events in eastern Europe and their intention of taking action after the war was over. Suggestions that Jewish communities or even individuals might be ransomed or even rescued from Europe were met with hostility, either on the grounds that the Nazi government might take an opportunity of intruding agents into Allied countries or else that it savoured of trading with the enemy. When individuals did manage to escape from the Balkans they were either put into internment camps under heavy guard or even returned to Nazi control. Jews who reached the Swiss border were almost invariably returned to the Germans and even Spain did not guarantee safe haven.

The outstanding instances of attempts to ransom large communities were in the case of Slovakia and Hungary. The Slovakian Government under Father Tiszo was fully prepared to sell its Jews, to either Germans or the USA. An initial offer by the American Joint Distribution Committee proved attractive enough to halt intended deportations to Auschwitz but German pressure eventually led to their resumption. In Hungary the Jews had initially been protected by the Horthy Government, and so long as Hungary remained a loyal ally of the Germans no action was taken. But the fear that the Hungarians might begin negotiations for a surrender led to decisive German intervention and by the spring of 1944 Hungary had fallen under full German control. By this time Eichman had determined on the removal of the Hungarian Jews, the last significant Jewish community in Europe. Its fate had been planned in advance, for the winter had seen an important expansion of extermination facilities at Auschwitz.

Eichman ordered the concentration of the Hungarian Jews into various regions and one after another these regional groups were despatched to Auschwitz. But in the summer of 1944 he made various offers through the Joint Distribution Committee and through one of the members of the Hungarian Jewish committee, Kastner. To the JDC he offered to sell the Jews of Hungary (or even at one stage all the surviving Jews) for several million dollars. To Kastner he made the offer of exchanging 'Jews for trucks' - all the Jews of Hungary in exchange for lorries that would be used only in Eastern Europe. As a token of 'good faith' he not only suspended deportations in progress but offered to release a trainload of Hungarian Jews, nominated by Kastner. The offer of such trainload was in fact made good, but the Allies refused to entertain any acceptance or even detailed discussion. To provide transport to the Germans for use on the Russian front (and thus antagonise the Russians) was hardly a conceivable prospect at the time when the Allies' Second Front had just been opened and relied upon continuing Russian pressure on German armies in the East, but the JDC protested strongly against its being forbidden even to try and spin out negotiations and keep the Germans talking.

It was this episode which however also raises the issue as to whether the Allies were really serious in seeking to rescue large numbers of Jews from Europe. Official comments scribbled on the margins of official despatches suggesting that the Allies would not have know what to do with a million rescued Jews leave an impression that there were many who were not too unhappy at the collapse of such talks, and there is no official hint that they might be continued in the hope that they might ascertain as to whether Eichman could actually have been able to deliver on his promises.

The Warsaw uprising. German soldiers rounding up Jewish underground members for deportation April-may 1943.

It was in Hungary however that there developed one of the best-known 'rescue' episodes - that based upon the activities of Raoul Wallenberg, the Swedish diplomat in Budapest who issued thousands of protecting papers for the benefit of Hungarian Jews who otherwise would have been deported and threw the protection of the Red Cross over a number of 'safe houses' in which others found refuge. Evidence is now coming to light about a myriad of officials all over Europe who, often enough against the direct orders of their own governments, issued papers to as many as they could find some quasi-legitimate reason. Spanish and

Above: SS troops walk past a block of burning housing during the suppression of the Warsaw ghetto uprising. The original German caption reads: An assault squad

Opposite: Nazis take captives at the end of the rising.

Portuguese consuls in particular tried to give papers to Jews of Iberian provenance, even if that had been many generations earlier. The Japanese consul in Kovno facilitated rescue papers for a Lithuanian yeshiva (rabbinical seminary) which found itself transferred through Russia to a new home in Japan and then Palestine.

All these activities, as well as of those who looked after individuals in hiding all over Europe – even in Berlin itself – point to one outstanding feature of these years. No Jew could survive in Europe by his (or her) own efforts. Anyone who survived did so as the result of the desire by non-Jews to take risks and to save a life.

Top: Jewish resistance fighters captured by SS troops during the Warsaw ghetto uprising. Warsaw, Poland, April 19-May 16, 1943.

Below: Juergen Stroop (third from left), SS commander who crushed the Warsaw ghetto uprising. Warsaw, Poland, between April 19 and May 16, 1943.

Top: German soldiers capture Jews hiding in a bunker during the Warsaw ghetto uprising. Warsaw, Poland, April-May 1943.

Left: Inhabitants of the Warsaw ghetto hide in a bunker during the uprising.

Above: Jews captured by the SS during the Warsaw ghetto uprising are interrogated beside the ghetto wall before being sent to the Umschlagplatz. The original German caption reads: 'Search and Interrogation.'

Top: SS soldiers pause to eat during the suppression of the Warsaw ghetto uprising.

Above: A German gun crew in action during the suppression of the Warsaw ghetto uprising.

Above: An SS soldier searches a captured Jewish resistance fighter during the suppression of the Warsaw ghetto uprising. The original German caption reads: 'Pulled from a bunker.'

Left: Jewish resistance fighters being interrogated.

Above and Left: Jewish resistance fighters in the forest Below: Jewish partisans, who were part of the Kovno ghetto resistance, are pictured in the Rudninkai forest near Vilna, just after the liberation. Pictured from right to left are Gafnowich, Zemec, Alte Tepper, Moshe Sherman, Berl Shtern, Rivka Bloch, Eliezer Zilberis, Yakov Rottner, Asia Shtram, Shimon Bloch, and others. 1944.

Above: Nazis shell a ghetto.
Overleaf: Young girl from Westerbork, Holland, peering from a freight car en route to a death camp in Poland

Life in the Ghetto

ONE OF THE EARLIEST set of instructions by the SS concerning the treatment of the Jews in the occupied areas of Poland was for the concentration of Jews from the countryside into the larger cities. Once that process had been set in motion further instructions provided for the establishment in each of these communities of a Council of Jewish Elders, a Judenrat. The initial principle was that of 'spatial separation' between Jews and Poles. Broadly speaking Jews were intended to be 'decanted' into the Lublin area of Poland, being evacuated from elsewhere in Poland and Germany. One part of Poland was to be incorporated into the Greater Reich, the so-called Wartheland, and all Jews were to be removed from that area as quickly as possible; it was not practicable however there to clear the city of Lodz of all its Jews. Accordingly as early as December

1939 the decision was taken to establish a closed-off Jewish quarter, a ghetto. This was not to be regarded as a permanent solution of the 'Jewish question' in the city. As the administrator of the District affirmed: 'I reserve to myself the decision concerning the times and means by which the ghetto and with it the city of Lodz will be cleansed of Jews. The final aim (endziel) must in any case bring about the total cauterisation of this plague spot.' The establishment of this ghetto however was to presage the way in which other areas were treated. In practice the concept of a Lublin reservation proved impracticable and as an alternative a number of ghettos all over Poland were created. Some of them were comparatively small, but others, especially Warsaw, were substantial and formed an important part of the German administration of Jews in Poland.

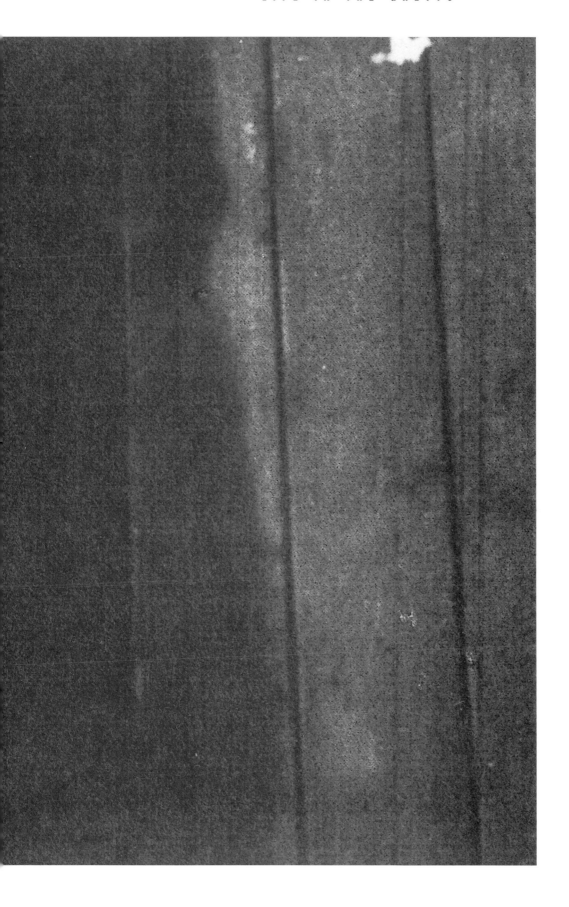

Theoretically each was managed by its own Judenrat, but it had been clear from the beginning that these bodies were 'fully responsible, in the literal sense of the word for the exact and prompt implementation of directives already issued or to be issued in the future'. Often enough the Chairman was to become an unwilling tool of the German governor as in Lodz for example where the chairman, Mordecai-Chaim Rumkowski, was given the trappings and appearances of power but in turn had no alternative but to cooperate with the most brutal instructions given to him, even when they involved the seizure and deportation to the death camps of all the children under ten years of age.

A great deal is known about these ghettos. In Lodz and Warsaw, just as later in Vilna or Kovno, there were scholars who conceived their task to be to describe the every day life of the inmates of the ghetto. Through these accounts we can see the pain of their life, the problems of finding enough food to keep alive, and the problems facing the ghetto leadership. For their part the members of the Judenrat tried to make life bearable for the inhabitants of the ghetto and to maintain such social institutions of the ghetto as hospitals, orphanages, and old age homes. Often the Council faced opposition not only from the Germans but also from elements inside the ghetto itself. In Warsaw for instance the head of the ghetto council had great difficulty in balancing the demands of some of those in the ghetto who saw only their own interests against the needs of the community as a whole. And also in Warsaw there were deep political divisions between the left-wing Bundist parties and the Zionist youth groups. Pictures taken in the ghetto, sometimes by its inhabitants and sometimes by the Germans, illustrate clearly the privations. They show bodies left lying in the streets and the death carts sent out to pick them up for burial; they show orphaned children begging for scraps and the work parties that had been sent outside the walls of ghetto being searched on their return in case they were smuggling food back for their fellows.

Basically the Germans saw the ghettos as merely an interim stage on the road to the destruction of the Jews of eastern Europe. The concentration of the Jews into what was invariably the unhealthiest part of the town was almost certainly intended to lead to the deaths of many of the inhabitants from various diseases, usually brought on by malnutrition. For their part the members of the Judenrat felt that the only hope of survival for the members of the ghetto lay in making it indispensable for the German war effort. Then, it was reasoned, the Germans would see that it was to their own best interests to keep the ghetto alive. In each ghetto there was a programme of setting up workshops providing goods for the Germans in return for a certain quantity of food; indeed some of the Germans in overall charge of the ghetto saw opportunities of making personal profits and thus had a direct interest in maintaining the ghetto. But such approaches to questions of survival failed to allow for the essentially doctrinaire attitude of the German hierarchy, and even pleas from the Army itself, pointing out that there were numbers of skilled Jewish artisans who were essential for the continued efficiency of the Wehrmacht, failed to gain anything more than a strictly limited period of survival for individuals.

During the summer of 1942 German pressure built up to reduce the numbers of Jews, even those working for the German war effort. In Warsaw instructions were given to the Judenrat that it would have to nominate at least 8,000 Jews a day for 'resettlement'. The head of the ghetto committed suicide rather than implement that decree but within weeks the numbers in the ghetto had been reduced from some

300,000 to 30,000. Elsewhere smaller ghetto communities were completely destroyed, their inhabitants being sent to one or other of the death camps that had been established. In Lodz the head of the ghetto acquiesced in the order to send the children, the sick, and the elderly for 'resettlement' in the hope that he might thus save the rest, keeping at least some of the community alive. To some extent he succeeded; the Lodz ghetto was the last to be liquidated. In the meantime the flow of goods from its factories continued to supply the Army.

There was a bitter irony about all these activities. The records of the ghetto illustrate over and over again the intense desire to hang on to life in order to outlive Hitler by even half an hour. Even for those who were most active in making the services of the ghetto available for the

Left: Jewish woman in the Warsaw ghetto selling the arm bands which had to be worn by the ghetto inhabitants.

Germans there was no 'collaboration', for that presupposes a belief in an eventual German victory. None doubted that the Allies would eventually win, would indeed have to win. Nonetheless their only hope for even a limited survival lay in giving positive assistance to those for whose defeat they prayed.

None of these ghettos had clear ideas of what was happening to other populations elsewhere. Communications were difficult, and sometimes only the bravery of girl couriers kept up some sort of information service. Resistance was difficult, even in many cases futile for lack of weapons, so that it was eventually a mark of desperation that several groups amongst the Jews of Warsaw prepared to sell their lives dearly.

Once the Germans had attacked Russia and Russian occupied Poland they encountered another large Jewish population. As German armies went into action they brought with

Left: Emaciated woman in the Warsaw ghetto.

them special groups (Einsatzgruppen) whose task was not only to murder Jews themselves but to encourage local populations to murder local Jews. As a result of such actions Jewish communities in these areas (unlike the Jews in the western parts of Poland) had no illusion as to what faced them in the ghettos which the Germans now established, and the leaders in Vilna or Kovno faced the same dilemmas as their opposite numbers in Lodz or Warsaw. In Vilna Jacob Gens, who need not have gone into the ghetto – he had married a non-Jewish woman – felt it his duty to defend as many of his co-religionists as he could. His attempt to create all aspects of Jewish cultural and educational life did not prevent the destruction of the ghetto, while he himself disappeared into the hands of the Gestapo. In Kovno the ghetto elected for themselves a head of the ghetto – Dr Elkhannan Elkes – who refused to conform to the wishes of the Germans, even refusing to assist in any form of selection. When the Kovno ghetto was finally liquidated the surviving women of the ghetto were taken to a camp at Stutthof and the men to Dachau, a working and 'educational' camp rather than a death factory.

Left: In the Warsaw ghetto, Jewish children with bowls for rations of soup. Warsaw between 1940 and 1943.

Above: A Jewish woman eating her ration of soup that she received at the public kitchen in the Kielce ghetto. This photo was one the images included in an official album prepared by the Judenrat of the Kielce ghetto in 1942.

Above: Leon Rozenblat, chief of the Lodz ghetto police, leaving a warehouse in the ghetto. 1940 -42.

Left: A Jewish man and child at forced labor in a factory in the Lodz ghetto. Lodz, Poland, date uncertain.

A child vendor among those selling miscellaneous wares at the market in the Lodz ghetto Lodz, Poland, cira 1941.

Right: The dead being wheeled out. Very often in the ghetto, bodies were left lying in the street. This meant that survivors could continue using the ration cards of the deceased. This also indicates the desperation of the survivors in the ghetto by ignoring the customary respect for the dead. The bodies were collected regularly by members of the Burial Society who took them to the cemetery.

A group of pre-school children lined up with sacks in the Lodz ghetto.1940 -44.

Left: Inmates at forced labor in the brick-works at the Klinker-Grossziegelwerke Sachsenhausen, opposite the main camp.

Above: Jewish police in the Kolbuszowa ghetto are forced to pose for propaganda purposes to show how Jews beat one another.

One of the first steps in the Nazi plan to murder the Jews of Europe, the German authorities ordered the concentration and segregation of Jews into ghettos. Jews from smaller communities were transported into the ghettos of nearby towns and cities. The large number of people and the limited available space and resources resulted in severe overcrowding, starvation, and disease.

SURVIVORS
The Einsatzgruppen Killings

Perhaps the easiest way of understanding the story of the holocaust is to approach it from the individual's stories of survival. Here are two such stories which portray the sufferings of the individual and illustrate some of the details of the fates which awaited the rest.

Massacres were carried out by Einsatzgruppen in every village in Lithuania, eastern Poland and western Russia. One young mother, Rivka Yosselevska, from a small village near Pinsk, was one of the few people to survive. This is an extract from her account of her experiences given in court, in Jerusalem, at Eichmann's trial on 8 May 1961.

'We were told to leave the houses – to take with us only the children. We were always used to leaving the ghetto at short order, because very often they would take us all out for a roll-call. Then we would all appear. But we felt and realized that this was not an ordinary roll-call, but something very special. As if the Angel of Death was in charge. The place was swarming with Germans. Some four to five Germans to every Jew.'

Attorney-General: 'Then all of you were driven out, and were taken to this square – weren't you?' Witness: 'No, we were left standing in the ghetto. They began saying that he who wishes to save his life could do so with money, jewels and valuable things. This would be ransom and he would be

Left: Children playing in Theresienstadt.

spared. Thus we were held until the late afternoon, before evening came.'

Presiding Judge: 'And did the Jews hand over jewels and so on?'

Witness: 'We did not. We had nothing to hand over. They already taken all we had before.'

Presiding Judge: 'I see'.

Attorney-General: 'Yes. And what happened towards sunrise?'

Witness: 'And thus the children screamed. They wanted food, water. This was not the first time. But we took nothing with us. We had no food and no water, and we did not know the reason. The children were hungry and thirsty. We were held this way for twenty-four hours while they were searching the houses all the time – searching for valuables.

'In the meantime, the gates of the ghetto were opened. A large truck appeared and all of us were put on to the truck – either thrown, or went up himself.'

Attorney-General: 'Did they count the Jews?'

Witness: 'Yes – they were counted. They entered the ghetto again, and searched for every missing person. We were tortured until late in the evening.'

Attorney-General: 'Now they filled up this truck. And what happened to the people for whom there was no room in the truck?'

Witness: 'Those for whom there was no room in the truck were ordered to run after the truck.'

Attorney-General: 'And you ran with your daughter?'

Witness: 'I had my daughter in my arms and ran after the truck. There were mothers who had two or three children and held them in their arms running after the truck. We ran all the way. There were those who fell – we were not allowed to help them rise. They were shot – right there – wherever they fell.

'When we reached the destination, the people from the truck were already down and they were undressed all lined up. All my family was there – undressed, lined up. The people from the truck, those who arrived before us... .

'There was a kind of hillock. At the foot of this little hill, there was a dugout. We were ordered to stand at the top of the hillock and the four devils shot us – each one of us separately.'

Attorney-General: 'Now these four – to what German unit did they belong?'.

Witness: 'They were SS men – the four of them. They were armed to the teeth. They were real messengers of the Devil and the Angel of Death.'

Attorney-General: 'Please go on – what did you see?'

Witness: 'When I came up to the place – we saw people, naked, lined up. But we were still hoping that this was only torture. Maybe there is hope – hope of living. One could not leave the line, but I wished to see – what are they doing on the hillock? Is there anyone down below? I turned my head and saw that some three or four rows were already killed – on the ground. There were some twelve people among the dead. I also want to mention what my child said while we were lined up in the ghetto, she said, "Mother, why did you make me wear the Shabbat dress; we are being taken to be shot"; and when we stood near the dug-out, near the grave, she said, "Mother, why are we waiting, let us run!" Some of the young people tried to run, but they were caught immediately, and they were shot right there. It was difficult to hold on to the children. We took all children not ours, and we carried them – we were anxious to get it all over – the suffering of the children was difficult; we all trudged along to come nearer to the place and to come nearer to the end of the torture of the children. The children were taking leave of their parents and parents of their elder people.'

Presiding Judge: 'How did you survive through all this?'

Attorney-General: 'She will relate it.'

Presiding Judge: 'Please will you direct the Witness.'

Witness: 'We were driven; we were already undressed; the clothes were removed and taken away; our father did not want to undress; he remained in his underwear. We were driven up to the grave, this shallow . . .

Attorney-General: 'And these garments were torn off his body, weren't they?'

Witness: 'When it came to our turn, our father was beaten. We prayed, we begged with my father to undress, but he would not undress, he wanted to keep his under-clothes. He did not want to stand naked.'

Attorney-General: 'And then they tore them off?'

Witness: 'Then they tore off the clothing off the old man and he was shot. I saw it with my own eyes. And then they took my mother, and we said, let us go before her; but they caught mother and shot her too; and then there was my grandmother, my father's mother, standing there; she was eighty years old and she had two children in her arms. And then there was my father's sister. She also had children in her arms and she was shot on the spot with the babies in her arms.'

Attorney-General: 'And finally it was your turn.'

Witness: 'And finally my turn came. There was my younger sister, and she wanted to leave; she prayed with the Germans; she asked to run, naked; she went up to the Germans with one of her friends; they were embracing each other; and she asked to be spared, standing there naked. He looked into her eyes and shot the two of them. They fell together in their embrace, the two young girls, my sister and her young friend.

Then my second sister was shot and then my turn did come.'

Attorney-General: 'Were you asked anything?'

Witness: 'We turned towards the grave and then he turned around and asked "Whom shall I shoot first?" We were already facing the grave. The German asked "Whom do you want me to shoot first?" I did not answer. I felt him take the child from my arms. The child cried out and was shot immediately. And then he aimed at me. First he held on to my hair and turned my head around; I stayed standing; I heard a shot, but I continued to stand and then he turned my head again and he aimed the revolver at me and ordered me to watch and then turned my head around and shot at me. Then I fell to the ground into the pit amongst the bodies; but I felt nothing. The moment I did feel I felt a sort of heaviness and then I thought maybe I am not alive any more, but I feel something after I died. I thought I was dead, that this was the feeling which comes after death. Then I felt that I was choking; people falling over me. I tried to move and felt that I was alive and that I could rise. I was strangling. I heard the shots and I was praying for another bullet to put an end to my suffering, but I continued to move about. I felt that I was choking, strangling, but I tried to save myself, to find some air to breathe, and then I felt that I was climbing towards the top of the grave above the bodies. I rose, and I felt bodies pulling at me with their hands, biting at my legs, pulling me down, down. And yet with my last strength I came up on top of the grave, and when I did I did not know the place, so many bodies were lying all over, dead people; I wanted to see the end of this stretch of dead bodies but I could not. It was impossible. They were lying, all dying; suffering; not all of them dead, but in their last sufferings; naked; shot, but not dead. Children crying

"Mother", "Father"; I could not stand on my feet.' Presiding Judge: 'Were the Germans still around?'

Witness: 'No, the Germans were gone. There was nobody there. No one standing up.

Attorney-General: 'And you were undressed and covered with blood?'

Witness: 'I was naked, covered with blood, dirty from the other bodies, with the excrement from other bodies which was poured on to me.'

Attorney-General: 'What did you have in your head?'

Witness: 'When I was shot I was wounded in the head.'

Attorney-General: 'Was it in the back of the head?'

Witness: 'I have a scar to this day from the shot by the Germans; and yet, somehow I did come out of the grave. This was something I thought I would never live to recount. I was searching among the dead for my little girl, and I cried for her –

Merkele was her name – Merkele! There were children crying 'Mother!", "Father!"– but they were all smeared with blood and one could not recognize the children. I cried for my daughter. From afar I saw two women standing. I went up to them. They did not know me, I did not know them, and then I said who I was, and then they said, "So you survived." And there was another woman crying "Pull me out from amongst the corpses, I am alive, help!" We were thinking how could we escape from the place. The cries of the woman,"Help, pull me out from the corpses!" We pulled her out. Her name was Mikla Rosenberg. We removed the corpses and the dying people who held on to her and continued to bite. She asked us to take her out, to free her, but we did not have the strength.'

Attorney-General: 'It is very difficult to relate, I am sure, it is difficult to listen to, but we must proceed. Please tell us now, after that you hid?'

Witness: ' And thus we were there all night, fighting for our lives, listening to the cries and the screams and all of a sudden we saw Germans, mounted Germans. We did not notice them coming in because of the screamings and the shoutings from the bodies around us.'

Attorney-General: 'And then they rounded up the children and the others who had got out of the pit and shot them again?'

Witness: 'The Germans ordered that all the corpses be heaped together into one big heap and with shovels they were heaped together, all the corpses among them many still alive, children running about the place. I saw them. I saw the children. They were running after me, hanging on to me. Then I sat down in the field and remained sitting with the children around me. The children who got up from the heap of corpses.'

Attorney-General: 'Then the Germans came again and rounded up the children?'

Witness: 'Then Germans came and were going around the place. We were ordered to collect all the children, but they did not approach me, and I sat there watching how they collected the children. They gave a few shots and the children were dead. They did not need many shots. The children were almost dead, and this Rosenberg woman pleaded with the Germans to be spared, but they shot her.'

Attorney-General: 'Mrs Yosselevska, after they left the place, you went right next to the grave, didn't you?'

Witness: 'They all left – the Germans and the non-Jews from around the place. They removed the machine guns and they took the trucks. I saw that they all left, and the four of us, we went on to the grave, praying to fall into the grave, even alive, envying those who were dead already and thinking what to do now. I was praying for death to come. I was praying for the grave to be opened and to swallow me alive. Blood was spurting from the grave in many places, like a well of water, and whenever I pass a spring now, I remember the blood which spurted from the ground, from that grave. I was digging with my fingernails, trying to join the dead in that grave. I dug with my fingernails, but the grave would not open. I did not have enough strength. I cried out to my mother, to my father, "Why did they not kill me? What was my sin? I have no one to go to I saw them all being killed. Why was I spared? Why was I not killed?"

'And I remained there, stretched out on the grave, three days and three nights.'

Attorney-General: 'And then a shepherd went by?'

Witness: 'I saw no one. I heard no one. Not a farmer passed by. After three days, shepherds drove their herd on to the field, and they began throwing stones at me, but I did not move. At night, the herds were taken back and during the day they threw stones believing that either it was a dead woman or a mad woman. They wanted me to rise, to answer. But I did not move. The shepherds were throwing stones at me until I had to leave the place.'

Attorney-General: 'And then a farmer went by, and he took pity on you.

Witness: 'I hid near the grave. A farmer passed by, after a number of weeks.'

Attorney-General: 'He took pity on you, he fed you, and he helped you join a group of Jews in the forest, and you spent the time until the summer of 1944 with this group, until the Soviets came.'

Witness: 'I was with them until the very end.'

SURVIVORS

Sara's Story

Sara Erenhalt was sixteen exactly a month before the German invasion of Poland , on 1 August 1939. She survived the war and settled in Israel.

'Our family was very large. There were eight sisters and a brother. Along with others we made for Stanislawow. In accordance with the Ribbentrop-Molotov agreement, in 1939 the Germans took one side of Przemysl, and the Russians the other. The bridge on the river San was the frontier.

'My family returned to Przemysl with the Red Army and remained under their occupation.

'From our side we could see Jews with yellow armbands, on the German side. It was known that the Germans were oppressing the Jews, confiscating their property and enforcing the wearing of the yellow armbands, but human life was not yet threatened.

'Shortly before the German invasion of Russia, I married Leon Pater. I was eighteen.

'The war broke out in June 1941. The Russians before leaving blew up a munitions store. My parents, as well as many other Jews, fled with the Russians, towards Russia.

'Near Stanislawow they were surrounded by Germans and had to go back. Again the family was reunited.

'The Germans had now taken over the whole of Przemysl and were merciless towards the Jews. They began by murdering about 1,000 people, including the chief rabbi of Przemysl.

'Our material situation under the Germans became much worse. My father, a tall, strong man, worked at the mill. He brought home wheat grains which we ground in coffee mills and this was our basic food. We were starving.

'Jews were allowed to move about town only during certain hours, from 8 till 10 am. Systematic actions and deportations began.

'During one action my husband was taken to Lvov, to a labour camp in Janowska, from which few people ever came back. I was in touch with my husband with whom I was able to correspond through my aunt in Lvov who had Aryan papers.

'In July 1942 I had a baby. Normally in peace-time this would have been a joyous event in the family, but at that time I was unhappy because I had brought into the world a being who would have to suffer along with me.

'When my child was two weeks old a great deportation took place. We wondered how to save the child at least. We decided to put the child in a crèche which then existed in the ghetto and, if I were deported, my sister would look after it, who as a working person might be allowed to stay.

'There was another idea – to hide in the shelter which my father had prepared beforehand in the cellar of our house. But there was the danger that if the Germans found us they would shoot us on the spot, as they had done with several other families.

'I went to the square for deportation with my parents and four of my sisters. My mother was then forty-four, and my father forty-nine. My sisters were almost children then.

'As she sat in the square my mother was grieving that I gave the child to the crèche, although before that we were afraid that precisely because of the child they would shoot us both in the square.

'At this moment the children from

Prisoners from Buchenwald that have been taken into the nearby woods are shown shortly before their execution by the SS. Clearly there were no 'extermination facilities' in the camp.

the crèche were brought to the square. At first there was deathly silence, then loud despair. Nobody could understand that the Germans could show such endless meanness and bestiality towards tiny innocent children.

'When I got over the shock I stood up and approached the group of children. I picked up my child and fed it. At this moment I noticed my sister who stood outside the square. I turned towards her instinctively, wanting above all to pass the child to her. I really don't know why I was so lucky. No one from the German or the Jewish police stopped me.

'My sister pulled me out of the square. I gave her my child and wanted to return to the square. I had a strange feeling that I should be able to save my parents. But my sister did not let me return to the square. She hid me and the child in the bunker which my father had prepared in our house.

'The people in the square were taken to Belzec. Nobody came back from there.

At first there was a rumour that they were working there, and I believed it. Only in 1943 when I was sent to Auschwitz did I realize that none of those dear to me remained alive.

'In the meantime my husband, learning that I remained in Przemysl, escaped from Lvov, from the famous death camp, and walked to Przemysl on foot. He walked at night, and in the daytime hid in barns, in the hay.

'He stayed in the ghetto illegally and hoped in time to make his stay legal.

'At the time my job was sorting out clothes taken from the Jews before deportation, and we lived on that.

'The necessity to sell clothes often meant that my husband left his hiding place and went into town. I threw parcels with clothes out of the window at the pre-arranged time and my husband collected them, and sold them on the Aryan side.

'Once I threw out a parcel in the usual way. A Gestapo man standing on the other side of the wire noticed me. He rushed in in a rage. He said he had arrested a man who picked up a parcel and threatened to shoot everyone if nobody confess. I was sorry for those working with me. I believed that the Gestapo man would carry out his threat.

'As soon as the German left came Davidovitch, the head of the Jewish militia, and his deputy, Tajch. They demanded that the person who was guilty should confess, because otherwise there would be unpleasant consequences. Then I stepped forward and confessed. Everyone was amazed. I did not care any more. I believed that my husband had been taken, as the Jewish militia also maintained, although this was not so.

'My colleagues at work asked Kommandant Davidobitch to cover up the whole matter. It was quite exceptional that I was not denounced to the Germans. They explained to the Gesatapo man that this parcel of clothes was meant for the children in the crèche, which had opened again.

'I was transferred, as punishment, to the non-working ghetto. There were two ghettos in Przemysl – one for those who worked and one for those who did not.

'The thought about my child gave me no peace. We spent all our time trying to find a way to save our child.

'My husband decided to leave the child with Poles. In order to do this he escaped into the Aryan side one day. He was noticed by the military police and arrested. They put him in prison.

'In May 1943 my husband was let out of prison. He was escorted by a Gestapo soldier and a Jewish policemen. My husband evidently knew that he was being taken to his death. He threw himself at the German and knocked the revolver out of his hand, but at that moment the Jewish policeman came to the German's aid and my husband was shot in front of everybody. He was then twenty- four years old.

'This was the only time in Przemysl that a Jew showed resistance and did not

Two young children wear the star of David.

passively go to his death, like everyone else.

'In September 1943 the ghetto for the non- workers was disbanded. At that time I was still with three of my sisters and my brother. My eldest sister was twenty-five. She was with her husband and her eighteen-months-old child.

'The action took us unawares in the night, but we still managed to hide in a previously prepared shelter. It was dug under an enormous house. Here were three shelters with seventy-five people. The Germans immediately discovered two of the shelters. Fortunately they did not find the third shelter where we were hiding.

'After the action we found ourselves in the bunker with no food, no light, and wearing only our underclothes. When things quietened a little our friends brought us bread and candles. They told us to stay until it would be possible to leave the shelter.

'Already before going down into the shelter my child who was then fourteen months old was ill and exhausted from starvation. I had no suitable food for him then, and staying in a dark airless place helped to kill my child. It died of suffocation. They carried me out unconscious.

'The child's death was a terrible blow for me. Life had no value. I wanted to die, but before that I wanted to revenge myself on the Germans. I got in touch with a group of five boys who had decided at any price to reach the partisans. On the day, the boys left early, but my sister did not wake me up and so prevented me from going with them. I stayed. None of those boys got back.

'It transpired that more than a thousand people had saved themselves this time in various hiding places. It was impossible to remain in the shelter any longer.

'My sister with her child, and another thirteen- year-old sister, went to the Aryan side to some Poles who promised to help them. The German police found them and returned them to the ghetto.

'I went over to the working ghetto. At that time the streets were covered with corpses and the Germans were shooting all the time. I walked and prayed that I might be shot in the back and have done with all this.

'In the working ghetto I was employed in the kitchen, but illegally. I was pleased with this job, because I could pass a little food to those hiding in the bunker.

'At that time I was looking after an eighteen- months-old child, whose parents were working for the Germans. I slept with this child in the cellar.

'The Germans realized that a lot of Jews were still hiding in bunkers and in order to flush them out they announced that they would employ the young in labour camps and put the old ones in old folks' homes.

'I, too, wanted to report there, but the kitchen workers did not let me. During a search I hid one more girl, Hinda Krebs, under planks which stood in the kitchen, against a wall.

'This was supposed to be voluntary reporting to the Germans, but the Germans searched every house and dragged people out.

'I was certain that my family was still hiding in the shelter. Later I discovered that my sisters answered the Germans' appeal and left the bunker along with others.

'The Germans gathered everyone in the school. They undressed them, shot them on the spot, and buried them in a mass grave near the school.

'The shooting lasted two days. There was not enough room in the mass grave, so the Germans poured petrol and paraffin on the bodies and burned them.

'After that action the Germans employed a group of 200 people to clean up the non-working ghetto. I was also in that group. I was working legally by then. In one house I found three people who hid under a pile of clothes during the action. I found out from them that none of my family remained alive.

'During that action the rest of my family had perished, three sisters and my brother. I alone remained, out of such a large family.

'I was taken, too, by the end of September 1943, during the deportation of the working ghetto. There were about a hundred of us, mostly young people. We were taken to a camp in Szczebnie, near Krosno. A young man called Ela Sztryzener, a member of the sports organization "Hagibor" in Przemyl, was among us.

'During the journey Sztryzener kept up our spirits, tried to make us see clearly, and explained that we must all help each other because in that lay our only chance of survival. At the end of his speech we sang Hatikva and we felt encouraged to face further struggles and an unknown fate.

'We arrived at Szczebnie. We found there Jews from Rzeszow, Tarnow, Bochnia, Wieliczka and also from Cracow and Przemysl.

'When we had been there for three days the Commandant of the camp, Grzymek, arrived and during the roll-call announced that he was now sending us to a resort where we shall be more comfortable than ever before. We discovered only later how much sadism and irony his words contained.

'We were taken on foot to the railway station. During the journey the Gestapo men pushed us and beat us with rifle butts.

'A goods train was waiting at the station. We were told before embarking to take off all our clothes and shoes and remain in our underclothes. They pushed us into the trucks like cattle, 200 per carriage. It was difficult even to stand. They closed the doors. We moved off.

'We did not know where we were being taken, but each of us had a foretaste of death.

'Among us was a woman who miraculously managed to board the train fully clothed. She was persuading me to run away, saying that she had some money with her which would help in our escape. She gave me her satin overalls.

'I felt completely resigned. None of my family were alive and life had no meaning for me. I had no strength left to make a decision and the escape did not materialize.

'We travelled for two days and two nights. It was stuffy in the train, there was no air to breathe. On the carriage roofs guarding the transport sat armed Gestapo men. After two days there were corpses in every carriage. They brought us in the night to the camp at Auschwitz. At the station we were told to disembark. In the light of a solitary lamp we looked like ghosts, with dishevelled hair, wearing only shirts, with tired faces.

'We were told to form groups of five. A group of Gestapo men stood there with the famous Mengele. He personally segregated the newly arrived people, placing some on the left and some on the right.

'I joined a group of 18 to 20-year-old girls. I thought that being with them would help me. I don't know what factors influenced them at the selection.

'I was sent to the right and the remaining group of girls to the left. Walking away I was certain that I was walking to my death. I looked back, towards the left, at the other group. I noticed in that group small children who were being put into lorries. Apparently they were told that they would have to go a long way and that was why they were being given a lift. But by then everyone knew that they were going to be killed.

'You could hear terrible screams from there, people were struggling before going into the lorries.

'All along the way I thought that it was because of the satin overalls that I was in the group of those still living.

'Our group was formed and we

were led or rather, driven, at night, over stones and gravel. it was about three kilometres from the station to Auschwitz. We were half dead when they led us into barracks and we were called in alphabetical order to be tattooed.

'I was given number 66952 and during many months I was given only a number. Later we were told to undress completely and were taken to the bathhouse. After the bath we had our heads shaven and were given some kind of rags for clothes. To these clothes we had to stitch the star of David.

'The clothes were given to us by Jewish women prisoners, mainly from Czechoslavakia. They beat us horribly for the slightest reason. They were cross that we arrived without clothes or shoes and that they couldn't take anything from us. Maybe also because they resented it that we had, according to them, lived a life of luxury until now, sleeping on featherbeds, while they had already suffered eighteen months in this place.

'In new clothes, with shaven heads we looked so strange that we hardly recognised each other.

'SS-man Hessler came and told us that he managed to get for us excellent work in the "Union" factory, but that we must first go through quarantine. We already knew that quarantine meant 90 per cent dead.

'Out of the 1,500 women brought here, only 350 were taken into quarantine.

'We were led into a barrack which was inside a huge camp, surrounded by electrified wire fences.

'We were placed in a barrack with wooden bunks. In every bunk there were twelve women, each sleeping with her head by her neighbour's feet, only in this way was there room for all of us.

'Near this barrack there was the hospital. Mostly Jewish women worked there, and their supervisor was a German woman, a political prisoner. We came out only to be counted, this took hours, and they kept counting us.

'There for the first time I came across Jewish women from Greece, Italy and France. The Greek women were covered with boils. They were all taken to the crematorium.

'After two days I met a girl I knew from Przemysl, Birenbaum. She was caught on the Aryan side and taken to Auschwitz.

'She pointed to the smoking chimneys of the crematorium and told us that we, too, were meant for the ovens, but until then we must be loyal to each other and help each other; then it would be easier for us to bear the suffering.

'Immediately after arriving I managed to pick up dermatitis. I had no medicine. I was very worried. I knew that Mengele paid special attention to full and clean bodies during the selections.

'I told my friend Birenbaum about my worry. She told me to rub the infected spots with ordinary wire. I listened to her advice with disbelief, but this really did help me, and saved me.

'Once a week we were taken to the bathhouse. There stood a German woman with a truncheon who rained blows at random at the naked bodies. In order to escape the beating I did not undress, and for two months I had not washed at all. All I did was drink the water in the bathhouse which was forbidden.

'By now we all had either typhus or bloody diarrhoea. Every day there were several dead bodies in our block. Some of the girls volunteered to carry the bodies into the trucks. For this they received a piece of bread. I never did this. I preferred to starve.

'Those women who survived the quarantine were transferred to the working camp "B", and from there they walked to work in the "Union" factory. The "Union" factory was three kilometres from Auschwitz. They made there fuses for guns.

'We were woken up at 3 am. Then

Jews being despatched on cattle trucks to camps.

we had the roll-call which lasted until 6 am. Then accompanied by Gestapo men and dogs we were taken to the factory. We worked 12 hours a day, with only two breaks of 15 minutes.

'In the morning we were given tea with bromide, at lunchtime water, which was called soup. At 9 pm we were given a piece of dry bread. The Germans added bromide to everything we ate, so that we would be confused and drugged. Indeed, people became daily more and more apathetic, without energy, with no will to live.

'At the factory there worked with me, on the same machine, a Jewish girl from France, Rachel, I do not remember her surname. She was born in Poland and left for France with her parents as a child. We became friends, we spoke Yiddish. After a while she began to trust me and introduced me to the underground organization. We were organized into groups of five. I knew only the girls in my five. But we did not know each other's names.

'Rachel told us what was going on in the world. She gave us courage, saying that the Red Army was approaching.

'Our main task was to accumulate as much explosive material as possible, i.e. petrol, paraffin, and also scissors.

'Our main objective was to tell everyone that we are all going to die in the crematorium, and when the Germans come to take us away we must set fire to the barracks, cut across the wire fences and allow at least a few of us to escape, so that the world would learn what goes on in the extermination camps.

'I stole scissors, and one of the girls hid them in the ground under her cot.

'I remember that during this period, during tongue examination, one of my friends, Tema Laufer, from Przemysl, who had just got over typhus was seen to have a white tongue and was taken to the sick bay. No one ever returned from the sick bay. She managed to hide several times during selection.

'But I was convinced that she was no longer alive. One day I received a note from her saying that she got out of sick bay, that she was in a so called "recuperation hut", but was covered with lice, had no medicine and needed help.

'By then I was already in touch with the men's camp. There were boys from Przemysl there, Dawid Sztolc and Irek Warhafrig who were earlier members of the Zionist group, Hashomer Hazair. I told them I needed ointment, to treat dermatitis.

The boys got the cream and once on a free Sunday (we had one Sunday off in every five weeks) I got into Block "A", to Tema. She looked like a real skeleton covered with boils. I treated her with the cream and left her to rest.

'After a while Tema got rid of the boils and returned to work in the "Union" factory. Tema Laufer is at present in Israel.

'When we were coming back from visiting Tema, I and a group of girls who were also visiting their friends, it was already dark. The gate of camp "A" was closed. Only now we realized what risk we were taking. How could we get back to our camp "B"?

'Fortunately there was a bombing raid that evening and all the lights were out. The girls, without thinking, began to climb the three metre high gate, bristling with electrified wire. We got across by a miracle. Suddenly the lights came on. The German policewoman cruelly beat those girls whom she managed to catch at the last moment.

'At the beginning of 1944 they were still bringing in Jews from Poland, and then they burned them alive without any selection.

'At these times we were locked in our hut so that we would not witness what was going on around us.

'Later on, when they brought Jews from Hungary, we were allowed to move about the camp, so that the newly arrived Jews would see that there were living people around. The Germans told the people sent to the crematorium that they were taking them to the bathhouse.

'At that point our group, which was working at "Union" was transferred to a barrack which was near the men's camp, a few kilometres away, towards the town itself. Here the conditions were a little better. It was possible to have a wash after work. But the food was the same.

'We lived in a brick building. We slept on decent cots and we even had blankets. Before us, the barrack had been inhabited by SS men.

'We now often had some help from the men, who would often pass to us a little food.

'From this camp it was only a kilometre and a half to the factory. The road was specially built, with barbed wire on either side.

'Our camp at Auschwitz had an experimental block. The experiments were mostly carried out on Jewish women from Greece. One would see these mutilated and disfigured women, without breasts, without thighs. They also took women for artificial insemination. Sometimes after carrying out the experiments they sent the women to us, to the camp. They were like living corpses.

'By the end of 1944 one crematorium in Auschwitz was blown up. It was the work of men who were engaged in the underground organization. The explosives which they used came from the "Union" factory.

'At the factory two girls, Estusia and Regina Sofirsztajn, from Bedzin, had worked with explosives. Regina worked as a foreman. It was they who stole the explosives and passed them into the men's camp.

'The Germans carried out an investigation and found out that the explosives came from "Union". They arrested Estusia. For two weeks she was kept in a dungeon and tortured. Later three more girls were arrested. They were subjected to terrible tortures. One of them Jadzia Gerther, broke down and named the others.

'They arrested all five, including Regina, and later they were hanged in front of all the women who were working at' 'Union". I was also a witness of this terrible deed.

'The girls walked to their deaths semi-conscious, beaten and tortured. One of the girls, before she died, cried out: "Hold out, their end is near!" She died with the last word: "Revenge!" on her lips. Estusia had a sister in the camp called Hanka. During the execution a woman overseer held her and forced her to watch her sister's death...

'The bodies of the five girls were left hanging all night. At every opportunity the Germans said we should take a good look at them, because the same awaited us. All this happened six weeks before liberation.

'We were all nervous and tense. We could not know whether the Germans knew about the other girls. We lived in incessant fear. It seemed a pity to perish now, when the end of our suffering was in view.

'We knew the end of the war was near and the Germans too realized their defeat. They were hurriedly removing people from Auschwitz, leaving only the sick. Daily more and more Germans disappeared from the camp.

'We, factory workers, expected to be taken away at any moment. We made use of the general confusion and stole dresses and scarves from the clothing store. We began constantly to wear the dresses under our striped uniforms.

'One day the Germans took us – it was the 18th of January 1945, and the men as well, to the transport, straight from work and without any food. There was not enough room for us in the carriages. We were taken on foot in the direction of Germany.

'Only a few Germans escorted us. We were better organized, and we could have disarmed them without difficulty. But we were afraid of the local Poles.

'We walked for twenty-four hours. We were tired and hungry. We suffered from the cold, we had no shoes, it was minus 18°. The people could hardly walk, they dragged along. The Germans pushed us with rifle butts. Anyone who fell behind was shot on the spot. There were many victims along the way.

'I walked in a group of five girls from Przemysl. All the time we were only thinking how to break away and escape. We tried to stay in the last ranks.

'Our five were: Genia Ekert, Tema Laufer, Tusia Zak, Stefa (whose name I cannot remember) and I. Two sisters from Jaroslaw joined us.

'Along the way the Germans ordered a stop in the village of Poreba. They allowed us to find a night's lodging in the peasants' houses, saying that at 5 am we must be present in order to continue on our way.

'We all walked into one of the houses. Inside was a little old man. We greeted him with the traditional Polish Catholic greeting (Niech bedzie pechwalony Jesus Chrystus). We asked him to let us sleep in the barn. He replied: "You poor orphans, how can I let you sleep in the barn in eighteen degrees of frost?"

'It turned out that our host was a priest. He wore secular dress. We began to talk to the priest and asked him to hide us in his house. He immediately agreed to hide me and Genia. Genia looked like a peasant and introduced me as her daughter. We convinced the priest that we could not be separated from our friends, that we were always together in the camp, that they would perish on the way.

'The priest hesitated. He was probably afraid of the Gestapo men who were quartered in the same house, and he must have heard them remind us that we must march on in the morning.

'The priest knew that we were hungry

and explained that the housekeeper could not manage to prepare food for all of us. Genia and I suggested that we would help out. He agreed. He allowed us to sleep in the barn on the hay and pointed out that we must not leave the barn until he allowed us.

'In spite of tiredness we could not sleep. In the morning we heard the whistles and calls of the Germans. But we stayed in the barn.

'One day we heard a loud conversation in Russian. We were certain the Soviets had come, and we were on the point of leaving our hiding place. But they were Ukrainians - members of the Vlasov army.

'There came two days' silence. The bombing stopped. Russians arrived.

'The first Russian who came into the priest's house turned out to be a Jew. I, who knew Russian, spoke to him and asked him if he was a Jew. He answered impatiently "What business is it of yours?" But when I told him that I was Jewish and that apart from me there were six more Jewish women there, he was amazed. He told us we had nothing more to fear and that we were the first Jewish women he had met at the front.

'He told us to leave immediately because there would be more fighting. On the following day we followed the Russians to Cracow.

'The priest wanted us to stay and said it did not matter that we were Jewish, what mattered was that Guardian Angels had sent us to him and that he had saved human lives. He also said that if we didn't find our families we could always go back to him and he would find us work. We had stayed with him for three and a half weeks.'

Prisoners of Auschwitz greet their liberators after 27 January, 1945.

'The Jewish State' a ship bringing Jewish survivors to Palestine, after capture by the British navy, October 1946.

The Aftermath

THE END OF THE WAR found a comparative handful of survivors, some 300,000. Some in the various Baltic republics or eastern Poland had been deported by the Soviets to the Russian interior and thus ironically had been saved from the Nazis. Some had lived through the camps or had not yet been caught up by the Nazi machine. Few were in their home countries but instead were increasingly concentrated into 'Displaced Persons Camps'. Their fates and eventual future homes were to become the plaything of international politicians and the whole issue of the future of Palestine, the Holy Land, the Jewish National Home. Few of the countries from which they had come really wished to see their return; few of them wished to return to the homes which had seen the murder of all their families and the destruction of their patterns of life. What had been destroyed of course was not merely more than six million individuals but over fifty thousand Jewish communities, large and small. Jewish life which had lasted for over six centuries was brought to an abrupt and violent end. In the past devastation of Jewish life had not been total and life had eventually resumed. That was no longer possible and if there were to be any renewal it would have to be in a different land, indeed in a different continent.

Above: Death mask of Henrich Himmler, who committed suicide after being captured by
the advancing British Army in 1945.

Above: Local German girl being forced by American troops to view the consequences of Naziism.

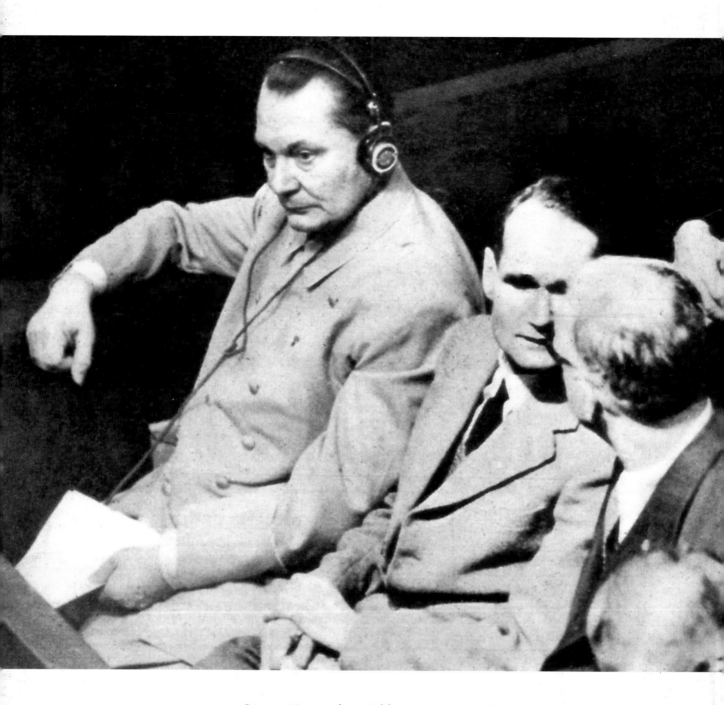

Göring, Hess and von Ribbentrop at Nuremberg.

Above: The former leaders of Hitler's Third Reich on trial in Nuremberg, Germany.
Front Row from Left to Right: Hermann Göring, Rudolf Hess, Joachim von Ribbentrop, Wilhelm Keitel, Ernst Kaltenbrunner, Alfred Rosenberg, Hans Frank, Wilhelm Frick, Julius Streicher, Walther Funk, Hjalmar Schacht.Back Row Left to Right: Karl Dönitz, Erich Raeder, Baldur von Schirach, Fritz Sauckel, Alfred Jodl, Franz von Papen, Arthur Seyss-Inquart, Albert Speer, Konstantin von Neurath, Hans Fritzsche.

Suggested Further Reading

Y ARAD *The Pictorial History of the Holocaust*

Y BAUER *The History of the Holocaust*

J BRIDGMAN *The End of the Holocaust: the Liberation of the Camps*

L DAWIDOWICZ *The War Against the Jews*

M GILBERT *Final Journey*

M GILBERT *Never Again*

A TORY *Surviving the Holocaust*

L YAHIL *The Holocaust*

Acknowledgments

The United States Holocaust Museum
US National Archives
The Imperial War Museum
Yad Yashem
The Illustrated London News

'Sara's Story' printed in Martin Gilbert's *Final Journey*. Original in Yad Vashem's archives.
'The Einsatzgruppen Killings' printed in Martin Gilbert's *Final Journey*. Original given at the trial of Adolf Eichmann.